CATFISHING

A PRACTICAL GUIDE

CATFISHING

A PRACTICAL GUIDE

Simon Clarke

Foreword by John Wilson

THE CROWOOD PRESS

First published in 2008 by
The Crowood Press Ltd
Ramsbury, Marlborough
Wiltshire SN8 2HR

www.crowood.com

British Library Cataloguing-in-Publication Data
A catalogue record for this book is available from the British Library.

ISBN: 978 1 84797 001 5

Dedication
To my wonderful children, Alice, Michael and Hannah; sorry for being
shut away for many hours writing this.

Acknowledgements
I owe thanks to a number of good friends for contributing and assisting
with pictures: John Wilson (who also wrote the Foreword), Chris Wade,
Bob Warren, Graham Lawrence, Arnout Terlouw, Colin Bunn, Henry
Hansen, Ken Latchford, Kevin Midmore, Pete Shefford, Martin
Walker, Richard Garner, Trevor Pritchard and Keith Lambert.
All rig diagrams were drawn by the ever helpful Brian Atkins and
tackle accessories for some photographs were supplied by the tackle
shops: Raison Bros, Tackle Up and Yateley Angling Centre.
And many thanks to my mum for many hours of help.

Line-drawings by Brian Atkins.

Edited and designed by
OutHouse!
Shalbourne, Marlborough
Wiltshire SN8 3QJ

Printed and bound in Malaysia by Times Offset (M) Sdn. Bhd.

CONTENTS

FOREWORD

I have known Simon Clarke now for possibly more years than even he cares to remember, and certainly since his formative, early teens when he and our mutual friend Keith Lambert used to travel up to Norfolk from their then Hertfordshire homes to fish my local stretches of the river Wensum for big roach and chub. And I've been privileged in watching their angling careers blossom ever since. In fact, their dedicated and professional running of the Catfish Conservation Group (CCG) during these past two decades has encouraged many anglers and fishery owners (myself included) to enjoy the spectacular fights of this exciting species. And I think catfish enthusiasts all over the country owe them an enormous debt; I certainly do. They encouraged me to stock catfish in my own two-lake fishery some 20 years back and I've accompanied the two of them every now and again on trips after wels catfish both at home and abroad ever since. Indeed, it was a research trip organized by Simon and Keith, together with our guide Gary Allen of the Bavarian Guiding Service, to the junction of the rivers Ebro and Segre at Mequinenza in eastern Spain which led to the filming of two of my *Fishing Safari* programmes for Discovery Television there, with weir pool catfish topping 100lb and beautiful common carp up to 30lb plus.

So it is with no small amount of pride that I pen this foreword to what I consider is not just a practical guide but a veritable bible for anyone who wishes to get into catfishing. As Simon so rightly points out, in the early days, before the CCG was formed in 1983, a mere handful of waters contained catfish. Now, over 400 stillwaters up and down the country have been stocked with wels catfish, and much of this achievement is owed directly to the hard work of those stalwarts in the CCG.

Being at the cutting edge of developing techniques during these last two decades, there is, in my opinion, no one more qualified than Simon to advise would-be catfishers on how to go about it all. He designs, develops and sells catfishing products for a living and has pursued big catfish all over England and Europe, and, whenever I ring up for a natter, where is he? Yes, out catfishing. So you the reader are in the very best of hands. Learn from the 30-plus specialized tackle-rig diagrams and over 150 colour photographs; marvel at the size that this truly fascinating, enigmatic species can reach, and the colour variations it comes in, when it has warm water and a glut of fodder fish to prey upon.

Good catting!
John Wilson 2008

INTRODUCTION

The Mysterious Wels Catfish

It's quiet, very quiet, the tree-lined lake calm and resting. In the pre-dawn haze, mist rolls across the lake's dusty surface. A small roach flips and skitters across the water. Bubbles betray fish movements beneath. Somewhere in the wood behind, the screech of a tawny owl breaks the silence. The angler lies quiet, waiting, hoping, expecting. Time passes inexorably, and dew drip-drips from the overhanging branches of a weeping willow. Far from the hustle and bustle of working life the angler finds solace, silence, serenity.

An intense scream cuts through the still air – a mechanical scream, an urgent demanding scream, constant and incessant. Then the scream stops, a whoosh, as the angler strikes and the rod hoops over. Out in the lake a resounding, solid, angry slap on the surface and the rod is almost wrenched from the angler's grip as the lighter groaning scream of the clutch signals catfish on! Welcome to the world of catfishing.

Three catfish are better than one!

Nick and his father Steve, with me holding the 21lb catfish that I caught during the filming of Nick Baker's Weird Creatures *programme about wels catfish at Withy Pool in Bedfordshire.*

The wels catfish is simply the biggest and hardest fighting freshwater angling quarry in the United Kingdom. A 10lb catfish fights harder than a 20lb carp. It is a fascinating, ancient fish, muscular, unpredictable and addictive. But despite being large, with big mouths, catfish are docile on the bank and easy to handle, so there is no reason to be afraid of them. Wels catfish have been in the UK for well over 100 years and are now more widespread than ever before. As little as ten years ago relatively few anglers had caught catfish, but now the greater availability of catfish fishing here and in continental Europe has enabled many anglers to encounter them. There are now over 400 waters in the United Kingdom containing wels catfish, so they are within reach of most anglers. For the more adventurous there are some huge catfish living in rivers and lakes in France, Spain and across Europe.

Anyone having the chance to fish for a wels catfish should jump at it. As I have heard from so many catfish anglers, 'One catfish and you're hooked!' They are tricky to catch, often unpredictable, something different that offers a real angling challenge. This book is intended to equip you to catch wels catfish here or abroad, with information and help on approach, tactics, tackle and baits, plus a lot more.

1 ALL ABOUT CATFISH

Wels Catfish

Identification

Wels catfish (*Silurus glanis*) – also known as sheat fish or silure – is elongated and scaleless with a strong upper body and a laterally flattened tail. It has a very small dorsal fin, with a small spine and four or five dorsal soft rays; it has one anal spine, and 90 to 94 anal soft rays; the caudal fin has 17 rays. It has paired pectoral fins, which have one spine and from 14 to 17 soft rays each. The paired pelvic fins are positioned behind the dorsal fin; each has one spine and 11 or 12 soft rays.

Wels catfish can be distinguished by their six barbules: two long ones on either side of the mouth and four shorter ones under the lower jaw. The sex can be determined in two primary ways: first, the flap of skin behind the vent in males is thin and comes to a point, whereas in females it is thicker and shorter; second, mature (7lb-plus) males typically have a thicker, rougher pectoral fin, with a rough leading ray (which becomes more pronounced in later spring as fish become ready to spawn).

The wels is usually dark on the top and the flanks with the belly paler. The fins are brownish. The body has a mottled appearance which is sometimes accompanied by brown spots.

Colour Variation

There can be great variance in colour; this is dictated by the environment. Typically, in clear water, the fish is very dark on the top and flanks

The pectoral of the male catfish: the first ray is thickened and the fin is large and scoop-shaped. This is particularly noticeable around spawning time.

The pectoral fin of the female is slightly smaller, with a smaller leading ray.

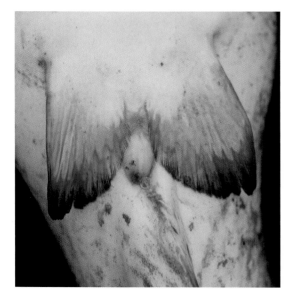

The female catfish has a short, fat flap of skin by the vent.

The male catfish has a long, slimmer flap of skin by the vent.

Clear-water catfish are generally dark with subtle colours.

with a white belly; in coloured (muddy) water the fish is normally pale. The wels can also change colour quickly – fish moved from a pale environment to a dark one can change colour within an hour. Catfish will also change colour when stressed, usually becoming paler and the flanks becoming redder. Any angler who lands a wels catfish must always closely monitor it for such signs of stress and – if any change of colour is detected – return the fish immediately.

Table 1 Typical length-to-weight ratios of wels catfish	
Length (m)	Typical weight (lb)*
1.6	60
1.8	80
2.0	100
2.2	140
2.4	180
2.5	210

* 'Typical' weights based on fish caught from France, Italy and Spain.

Size

How large catfish can grow has been the subject of much rumour and debate. There has been talk of fish over 400lb and of up to 600lb 'from Russia'. Personally, in over 25 years of interest in the species, I have never seen a picture of one over 240lb, though there has been a reliably sourced report of a fish found dead which was estimated at 300lb. The ultimate size will be debated endlessly, though the key fact is that the wels grows quickly in length up to approximately 2m and then this growth slows and the fish bulks up, so that a fish 2m long would normally be approximately 100lb in weight. However, a 200lb fish could be as short as 2.4m.

Many books will record maximum lengths of 3m for catfish, which is possible as an ultimate

Where it all began: Woburn Abbey is the scene of the first successful introduction of wels catfish into Britain.

length, and I would imagine a size of 300lb-plus would be feasible, though I am sceptical about 400lb being a possibility. Even at 300lb it makes the wels one of the largest freshwater fish in the world, and one of the most numerous to grow to over 100lb.

Size in the United Kingdom

Catfish have now been present in Britain for over 120 years and, to date, have not grown anywhere near as large as those in the more southerly climates of their natural range. Their exact potential and ultimate size in the UK present a confused picture because, during the time they have been here, many fish have been imported, so exact figures are impossible to determine. However, it has been reported – and believed – (though without photographic evidence) that when the Shoulder of Mutton Lake was drained over 40 years ago the fish removed were over 70lb.

Apart from that instance there are no reports of catfish any larger than the 43-08lb example caught in 1970 from the Tring reservoirs. Since that time catfish have become more widespread, and the type of water they inhabit – and the dramatic increase in carp fishing in particular – have changed the size profile of catfish: they have been stocked into many carp fisheries where there are vast amounts of anglers' baits now being thrown in every day, resulting in all species growing more rapidly than in the past.

When I started catfishing in 1984 a 20lb fish was a real achievement and a 30lb fish was fantastic; today 20lb is extremely common, as are 30lb-plus fish. Though there are now many more waters containing catfish, most of the waters that have contained them for 40 years or more have produced bigger fish in the last ten years than ever before. Today there are over 25 waters containing catfish of over 60lb and more than 50 with 40lb-plus fish. To determine the largest fish is difficult since there are a few waters in the country containing catfish of over 100lb, though all of these fish were stocked at over 100lb. Apart from these fish, the largest was 91lb, which was likely to be a fish imported at probably 5–10lb, and fish of likely full British heritage have been caught up to 60lb.

As a result of large fish being imported, there is no current official record for the UK. Listing of the record was suspended several years ago at

Table 2 Estimated number of British waters containing catfish over time

Year	Number of waters
1900	2
1950	6
1970	20
1987	50
1997	250
2007	400

Table 3 Estimated number of British waters containing catfish of 30lb and over

Year	Estimated total waters	Waters with >60lb fish	Waters with 40–60lb fish	Waters with 30–40lb fish
1970	20	0	1	3
1980	22	0	1	4
1990	35	0	4	8
2000	250	5	14	27
2007	400	25	58	83

We experimented with pheasant tags on Adams Pool, the CCG lake, to monitor fish growth. Unfortunately, while the tags stayed in, when the fish were caught the tags would easily be knocked out and so proved ineffective.

62lb. But I think it is likely that fish could reach 100lb in a water in the south of the country, where large amounts of anglers' bait are continually being put in (though this would not be commonplace as there are many waters where catfish growth rates are much too slow to reach that kind of weight). But to get an idea of the potential size of fish, we can look at the typical annual growth rates. These are:

- Poor, 2lb.
- Average, 3–4lb.
- Very good, 5–6lb.
- Exceptional, 6–8lb.

Very occasional annual growth rates of 10lb have been recorded, but never on a consistent basis – such statistics normally occur where fish have been introduced and may have been lean when first weighed and then filled out.

Range
Wels catfish is native to eastern Europe and Asia. It occurs naturally as far west as Germany and as far south as Iran. It has been introduced to many other countries, including France, Spain, Italy, England, Sweden, Turkey and the Netherlands. In the United Kingdom it is present in over 350 waters, primarily in the southern half of the mainland, with few waters north of Leeds.

Reproduction
Males pursue females just under the water surface. This is an indication that spawning will occur the same evening or the next day – usually the former and often before a thunderstorm on warm and stifling days. The male nudges the female in the anal region, swims under her and may lift her so that her back is above water. The male then wraps himself around the female for 10–12 seconds after which the male and female separate and the female sinks slowly to the bottom and discharges eggs, the male following to release milt (semen). This process can be repeated several times over one- to two-hour intervals with the result that the water around the nest becomes milky from sexual discharges.

The nest is made in shallow, 20–60cm deep, water. It is created by the male's pressing down in mud or weedbeds to form a depression in which the female then lays up to 400,000 adhesive, yellow eggs with diameters of around 2–3mm. The male guards the incubating eggs, even during the day, moving his tail fin every three to five minutes to ensure adequate oxygen supplies. The eggs hatch after three to five days.

Habits and Habitat

Silurus glanis is found in a wide variety of rivers and lakes across its range, and in many habitats it survives in river delta and estuary areas, tolerating brackish water. The fish is generally solitary, preferring quiet water, usually with a soft bottom such as mud. It may live in river bed holes, under bank overhangs or under other obstructions on river or lake beds, such as sunken trees. The fish is most active at night, though in coloured water it is active in the day. Catfish are also found in fast water in some rivers and have proved able to cope with a strong flow.

Diet

In natural conditions the wels catfish is a predatory scavenger, feeding on a wide variety of natural food, such as worms, snails, crustaceans, aquatic insects and small fish. At adult sizes it will also prey on crayfish, fish, frogs, rats and waterfowl. It uses the incredible suction created by its suddenly opening its large mouth to take in prey. Both the top and the bottom jaw have pads of inward sloping, soft teeth used to grab and hold prey. They then use their two pairs of crushing plates to soften the food before swallowing it.

Other Catfish Species

You may encounter catfish that are not wels. The other catfish species that are present in the United Kingdom and in some other European countries are uncommon and generally much smaller than wels catfish. Identification is usually an issue only if the fish are small (because distiguishing features are less obvious than they are in big specimens). There are three species that you may encounter.

During the spawning season catfish can be very aggressive; they often bite each other.

Aristotle's Catfish

There is one rare catfish closely related to the wels catfish, though you are unlikely ever to encounter one. Aristotle's catfish, *Silurus aristotelis*, is found only in and around the Akelhoos river system on mainland Greece. It is similar looking to a wels but can be identified by the fact that it has only four barbules, with just two under the lower jaw. Little is known about the size to which it grows. In theory, it should be able to grow large, being so similar to the wels catfish. One day I shall travel to investigate more about this sub-species.

The American channel catfish, Ictalurus punctatus.

Channel Catfish

The channel catfish (*Ictalarus punctatus*) is the other species that you are most likely to meet in Britain. It is a native of North America, with a wide range from Canada down to the southern USA. Channels normally inhabit rivers. They grow to around 60lb maximum, but rarely exceed 20. It has a small, underslung mouth and eight whiskers, four on the bottom jaw, two at the side, and two coming out from the top jaw. When small (under 8in) they often have spots on the flank which gradually fade as they grow. There have been many thousands of channel catfish imported into Britain over the last 20 years and sold through the pond and aquarium trade. Inevitably many of these have flourished over the years, grown too large for their owners and have been released into waterways across the country. This is illegal and should not be condoned. However, this has proved that channel catfish are not an invasive species since I know of no authenticated breeding of channel catfish here and, while many survive, grow and have subsequently been caught to low double figures, they do not appear to thrive.

The significance of the species is apparent when you are trying to find new catfish waters: reported wels captures may in fact have been channel catfish. If 'a few small catfish' are reported,

The channel catfish in albino form. Many channel catfish have been imported and sold as pond or aquarium fish.

but no larger fish, be suspicious and investigate further before launching a wels campaign.

Unusually among catfish species, the channel catfish is common in albino form and a large percentage of the imported channels have been albinos; so, if you hear of an albino catfish being caught in Britain, it is highly probable that it will be a channel catfish.

The American bullhead catfish, Ictalurus/Amierus melas.

Side by side, the wels catfish has the distinctive two long barbules, and none on the top jaw. Both the bullhead catfish (shown) and the channel catfish have two barbules on the top jaw.

Perfectly displayed: the whiskers or barbules of the wels catfish – two long ones at the side and four short ones below.

Bullhead Catfish

The bullhead catfish (*Ictalurus/Amieras melas*) is a nasty customer – it is aggressive and a prolific breeder, with the potential to affect fisheries adversely – and it should never be introduced. In France it has established large populations in lakes and rivers and has, as a result, become a major pest. Thankfully, it is very rare in Britain.

Indeed, I have not heard of any being caught in the last ten years. In the past, like the channel catfish, the bullhead catfish was widely imported for the ornamental fish trade in the 1970s and 1980s, but in the last 20 years there have been few in circulation and I have not seen one for a long time.

The bullhead catfish is small, growing to a maximum of 2lb (and usually only about 1lb);

Species	Whiskers: top jaw	Whiskers: lower jaw	Total	Other features
wels	2 long ones each side	4	6	tiny dorsal; small eyes
channel	2 at side, 2 on top	4	8	slim fish, large eyes; often albino
bullhead	2 at side, 2 on top	4	8	short stubby fish, small
Aristotle's	2 long ones each side	2	4	very rare; found only in Greece

Table 4 Comparison of catfish species for identification

The business end of a big cat.

it is shorter and more squat than the channel catfish and usually darker with a brown tinge, whereas the channel catfish tends to be slate grey in colour. The mouth is on the front of the fish and not really underslung or over-slung. In common with the channel catfish, it has eight barbules, four on the bottom jaw, two at the side and two on top.

It has particularly sharp spines in the leading ray of the dorsal and the pectoral fins; these contain poison and can cause painful injury if the fish is handled without care.

Other Catfish that Aren't Catfish

Occasionally, inexperienced anglers will report having caught 'catfish', but in some cases they are referring to miller thumbs or stone loach, which both look like a miniature catfish. However, since neither grows more than about 6in long the potential for confusion is limited.

There are a number of tropical species of catfish that could theoretically survive in our climate for some time, but I have never yet heard of any being caught by anglers.

2 CATFISHING IN THE UNITED KINGDOM

With over 400 waters containing catfish, most anglers wanting to target catfish now have a viable water within 40 miles of where they live. Though there are many areas of the country that have only a few waters, many counties are now well provided for. Among the waters containing fish there are a number of angling resorts and commercial fisheries with great on-site facilities for those willing to travel in order to fish a long session at a venue further from home.

The majority of the waters are in the southern half of the country. There are a reasonable number in the Midlands and some in the North and in Wales, but no viable fisheries in Scotland.

Finding Your Catfish

Stated simply, far and away the best source of information on catfish fisheries across the country is the Catfish Conservation Group (CCG). If you want full information on location, control, facilities, stock and cost then look no further than the CCG book *Guide to UK Catfish Waters*. The second edition of the book is now available from the CCG web shop at www.catfishconservationgroup.com, or by post (*see* Appendix II). It is also distributed to tackle shops through the supplier Catfish-Pro (*see* www.catfish-pro.com for a list of stockists).

Such guide books are notoriously hard to keep up to date so always use the book as a starting point and get latest information direct from the fishery, but it should help to narrow your list of potential waters, give you contact details and an idea of the stock. I have included a full current list of British waters compiled by the CCG and arranged by county as Appendix I. If you want a more up-to-date list of waters then purchase a copy of the CCG's annual magazine, *Whiskers* (free to CCG members); the list is the same format as in the appendix.

Bear in mind that the published lists of waters will never be completely accurate as there are a number of closed syndicate waters containing catfish, as well as newly stocked fisheries or waters from which fish may have been removed. So it is always worth using other sources of information such as the angling press (catch reports and fishery guides are most useful), the internet (but use carefully and sift the facts from the clutter), word of mouth, your local tackle shop, and the CCG and its website, magazine and meetings.

Catfisherman's Health Warning

Apart from the list of waters that are known, there may be others that contain catfish, and angling is rife with speculation and myths about them and their rumoured stock of, for instance, huge fish, albinos, and so on. To avoid frustration, depression – and possibly rage – carefully check any potential waters to verify the presence of fish before starting your campaign. If you just cannot be sure then I recommend occasional test sessions and the maximum use of prebaiting to increase your chances.

Is it a Wels Catfish?

If you hear reports of catfish in a new water, check that they are wels catfish. A large number of channel catfish in particular have been sold through the ornamental fish trade in recent

There are many magical places to fish – and some people don't understand why we go fishing …

years, and other species do turn up in lakes from time to time, usually as a result of someone discovering one in his pond or of one outgrowing an aquarium and then being dumped in a local lake. The releasing of any ornamental fish in this way is to be strongly discouraged. To aid identification, check the details in Chapter 1.

Rivers

The CCG list of waters contains details of rivers known to produce fish. Targeting fish in rivers is a real lottery since there are really no British rivers with sufficient stock to ensure the expec-

tation of a good catch rate. There is likely to be the odd, large cat in some, notably the Thames, but location is the issue. There have been many reports of catfish activity or fish lost from the Thames in particular, but I am sure that few of these were catfish. There have been catfish caught, the largest being one of 52lb in 2005, but captures have been few and far between, despite there being an increasing number of carp anglers on the river, whom I would expect to pick up a few if the population were bigger.

If you do want to try rivers then find out as much information as you can, and I would strongly advise you to invest time in prebaiting to maximize your chances of attracting fish to where you are. If possible, cooperate with some other anglers to cover a reasonable area of water. If you try, good luck!

Theoretically, it should be possible to catch river catfish in the United Kingdom by 'clonking' (*see* Chapter 7). However, a few of us have tried and I do not know of anyone catching a catfish by the method. Indeed, when Keith Lambert and I tried for two days on the Great Ouse we did not identify any catfish on the echo sounder, despite covering a huge area of water and some great looking areas. A few people have also tried clonking on the Thames with, as I understand, no action. I believe that this indicates that the catfish populations of these rivers are lower than many expect.

The scarcity of wels catfish in rivers also supports my view that they are not an invasive species: clearly they have not established significant populations and so do not represent a significant threat to native species. This view has been supported by the Centre for Environment,

Fisheries and Aquaculture Science (CEFAS), who believe that there is a greater threat from explosive population species such as the topmouth gudgeon. In fact, as detailed by CEFAS in 'Aquatic Invasions' (2007), the wels catfish is classified as 'rare' in the Thames after extensive surveying failed to locate a single fish. Hardly the cause for a national panic about catfish in rivers.

Lakes

Lakes are the way to go for catfishing in Britain.

Selecting Your Target Water
I think it is important to select carefully the water or waters that you plan to fish. When selecting waters my main considerations are:

- Location.
- Cost.
- Catfish stock – quantity and size.

One of the most unusual places I have fished for catfish is Naseby reservoir: a massive lake, with boats and a few catfish – blanking on this water was a doddle!

- Angling pressure – from cat anglers as well as other anglers.
- Aesthetics – the look of the fishery.
- Potential – could I gain in future by getting to know the water now?

I always look to fish a variety of waters during a season: a water I am familiar with and fairly local; a good water with big fish, maybe fairly expensive to fish; and a water with potential or uncertain stock that I will try out knowing that it is likely to be hard going.

The reason I vary the waters is that, from previous experience, I find that if you concentrate on a water that is too hard it can become dispiriting. When I first moved to north Hampshire in 1985 I had just started catfishing and had spent my first two seasons at the Airman Pit in Bedfordshire, where I caught a few. I checked the CCG waters list to find a more local venue. The closest water was 49 miles away – Vauxhalls Pit, at Stanton Harcourt, near Oxford. I fished the water for the next two seasons and didn't hook a single catfish (I fished a total of more than 25 nights), felt really burned out and dispirited, and came to realize that I go fishing to catch fish and had really had enough of blanking. So the following season I stopped fishing the water and spent a year fishing the Kennet for roach and just fished the odd CCG fish at Woburn Abbey. That season, I realized the need for balance. Ever since, I have fished a variety of waters and found it a good way to keep my enthusiasm going.

Each angler goes fishing for his own reasons and takes his own decisions. Some will fish a water only if it has a potential personal best, and others fish only their local water; to me, that is the great thing about fishing – it's about what you choose to do.

Preparation

Now you have selected your water, how will you catch your catfish? Good preparation helps to maximize your chances of catching.

Watercraft

In modern-day angling, watercraft does not have the prominence that it justifies. For many anglers who fish carp lakes that are heavily stocked and that produce good catch rates, watercraft is less critical than it is on the vast majority of other fisheries across the country. On rivers, watercraft is essential and will really make a difference.

So what is meant by watercraft? My interpretation is how you observe and 'read' a water, and how you use your observations and judgement to influence:

- The swim you fish.
- Where you believe your target fish are and where they will move to and patrol.
- What method and tactics you will use to target your fish.
- What bait and loose-feed tactics you employ.
- Where you position your bait.
- How you set up your tackle and swim.

My Approach

I ask myself the following questions:

- What do I already know about the water?
  Fishing a water from a completely cold start can be tough, particularly if there is a low catfish stock.
- Who can give me information?
  Fishery owners, bailiffs, and other anglers on the lake can all provide pieces of the jigsaw of knowledge that will give you some pointers and indicators, though information that is provided solely by other anglers should not be given too much importance: it should be judged alongside all other factors.
- Where have fish been caught from the water – which swims and areas?
  Catfish have shown a tendency on many waters to be caught from particular areas, so identifying these areas is useful.
- On what baits have fish been caught?
  Take particular care with this question: there is a big difference between catfish caught by anglers that are not actually targeting catfish, and baits that have proved successful with

anglers who *are* targeting catfish. For example, if boilies have accounted for several catfish, do some sums and work out the hit rate for carp anglers on the lake: how many carp rods are out and how many catfish have been caught on those rods? Then compare the answer to this with any information on catch rates for those who are truly targeting catfish; you may well find this enlightening. On a local water I have fished I worked out that there were at least 25 carp anglers to every one catfish angler. Though many catfish came out on boilies, the hit rate for targeted catfish was far higher when 'traditional' catfishing methods were used.

- What baits have other, non-catfish anglers been using?
  A significant percentage of most fishes' diet is anglers' bait, so if a water has received a lot of particular baits this can be a factor. For example, carp waters containing catfish are bound to have received high levels of boilies and pellet, fed in by the carp anglers.

- What level of angling pressure has there been? This can be important in order to ascertain the levels of bait that have been put in, plus how much disturbance there has been in the water and how it will affect the catfish's movements. On a busy water, with many anglers clumping round the bank with gear and setting up, the catfish movements are restricted during the day; they tend to feed much more at night when there is less noise and vibration on the bank. Additionally, if a water is heavily carp fished and bolt rigs have been extensively used, catfish will often become more sensitive to anglers' lines than on other lakes. The number of anglers will also affect the amount of bait going in and therefore how much of your feed you might lose.

When you arrive on the fishing day, get the latest news of recent captures, methods and baits. To complement any prior knowledge recent captures can be important, and often catfish will switch off or switch on. If fish have been caught recently they may well be on the feed.

Always check for any regurgitated food. In this case the catfish I caught on squid clearly had a taste for it and had also been feeding on perch fry.

Choose your Swim

When choosing your swim, take into account where others are fishing. I never like to fish an area that is 'cut off'. For example, I won't normally want to fish a bay if there is an angler on the neck of the bay with tight lines out. I will normally position myself away from other anglers, with at least one swim free on either side of me. If you simply cannot do this, choose a swim where you can position your baits in areas that are least affected by other anglers.

Read the Water in your Swim

Having chosen the swim, consider where you will position your baits. This may involve checking depths, thinking about where fish may be

Catfish look for places with cover in which to lie up. In this lake the catfish will almost certainly rest under the trees, feeling safe in the dark. Plan where to position your baits to intercept them as they come out to patrol.

lying up and patrolling, and identifying where any bait fish may be. If there are any snags in your swim, plan in advance how you intend to play the fish to avoid them if possible. Also plan how you will lay out your swim to keep organized, and decide where you will retain any fish caught, if that is required.

Choose your Method and Bait
Assess the weather conditions. In colder conditions, for example, I will fish livebaits closer to the bottom and use softer baits, such as luncheon meat. On a well-fished water I will fish a slack line, back lead or free line to avoid the fish spooking off the mainline. I may decide to fish a bait and method that has been successful on this lake on previous occasions but then try something new on the other rod.

Take Care Setting Up
I always set up back from the swim and as quietly as possible, particularly if I am going to fish close in. I have never – and would never – use a mallet to bang in any storm poles or bank sticks. Position your tackle and gear carefully and stay quiet.

You are well advised to note all these questions and points before you even cast a line into a water. Of course, you may well fish a water regularly and be familiar with it, but be prepared to experiment and to try different things. Many times an angler new to a water will fish it for the first time – in a different way from that of the regular anglers – and will catch well. Beware of the local 'expert' and take all advice with a pinch of salt. 'The catfish in this lake don't take X-Y-Z bait' is an assertion that I have heard expressed many times. Often it is sound advice, but not always. Fish feeding and behaviour also change over time in a fishery, so watch out for these factors, too.

Bait Positioning

Positioning your bait can be important. The diagram on page 28 shows a typical lake where I would be putting baits out. Use this as a guide to complement any other information you may have about where you are fishing.

Weather and the Time of Year

The metabolism of catfish is significantly affected by the water temperature. The higher the temperature, the faster the digestion rate and the more active they are. In cold weather they

Success on my first early April session, with water temperature 9.5 degrees: a 10-08 and a 25-08 – well pleased.

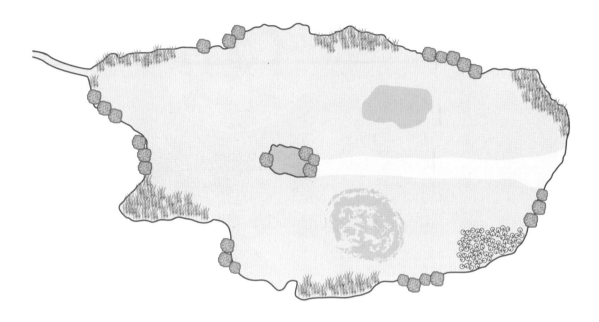

Bait positioning can be critical to increasing your catch rate. Here on a lake diagram I have given an idea of the positioning I would recommend for the several areas. This assumes that no other anglers are close by; if others are present you may need to alter the positions.

Swim A
Rod 1, position 1; close in next to overhanging bushes where catfish may lie up and patrol; as the position is close I would set up rods back from the edge of the lake and keep very quiet.
Rod 2, position 2; across to the reeds on the far side, with either slack line or back leaded to avoid the line's disturbing fish.
Rod 3, position 3; open water (normally a livebait position).

Swim B
Rod 1, position 3; open water livebait.
Rod 2, position 5; margin fished bait.
Rod 3, position 7; open water towards island, position can be varied to put closer to island, if within reach.

Swim C
Rod 1, position 6; margin fished by reeds.
Rod 2, position 7; open water, livebait.
Rod 3, position 8; close to island.

Swim D
Rod 1, position 9; margin fished by reeds.
Rod 2, position 10; open water, in deeper water, where catfish may lie up
Rod 3, position 11; close to overhanging bushes.

Swim E
Rod 1, position 12; margin fished by reeds.
Rod 2, position 13; open water, varying position between bar and deeper water.
Rod 3, position 14; close to lilies and margin cover.

Swim F
[Note: in this swim you should use heavier tackle because of weed beds, snags and narrow swim]
Rod 1, position 15; close to weed bed.
Rod 2, position 16; open water, close to or on bar.
Rod 3, position 17; margin fished near lily pads.

Swim G
Rod 1, position 18; margin fished by reeds.
Rod 2, position 19; close to island.
Rod 3; any open water position.

Even in early April, the fish will have been feeding, as is apparent from the fat stomach on this one.

have the ability to switch off completely to minimize loss of condition. So when is the best time to fish?

Spring into Action

A few years ago we would be waiting until late May and June to fish for catfish and very little early-season fishing was undertaken. That has changed in recent years with an awareness that there is good catfishing to be had during the early spring. How quickly individual lakes start fishing seems to vary: shallow, smaller and well-stocked waters seem to be the quickest off the mark, since I assume that they are quicker to warm up and the fish eat more anglers' baits than in large lakes. Monitor the temperature in your local waters, not right in the margins, which would usually be warmer, but out in more than 3ft of water. If the temperature is 9.5 degrees or above, get fishing! As with all fishing, the relative temperature change is also important, so a quick rise from 6 to 9 degrees may trigger an early feeding spell.

Soft baits are the order of the day for cool-water catfishing. Meat baits and worms have proved consistent in these conditions. Livebaits can work well, but you need to adjust your methods accordingly, fishing light polyball rigs close to the bottom as the cats will not chase them far. Do not be surprised if takes are finicky in cool water; the fish still put up a decent fight. You may also find that pike are a particular problem in cool water, so be prepared to adjust your tackle if this is the case.

Summer on the Surface

In May, as the weather and the water temperature warm, changing to livebaits will bring success. As the water gets warmer, position livebaits closer to the surface as the catfish will be feeding more actively and aggressively. To locate feeding areas, always watch out for any sign of fish striking. Meat baits and other soft baits will still work throughout the summer, though problems from nuisance fish will increase.

Depending on the type of fishery, you will probably find that coloured water and breezy conditions with a good ripple will enhance the catfish's confidence to feed close to the surface during daylight hours as well as at night. But

I had many happy seasons on Badshot Lea before a tragic problem with weed treatment resulted in a big fish kill that greatly reduced the catfish population.

you can look forward to five months of consistent catfishing between May and September.

Autumnal Slowdown
In late September and October, as summer gives way to autumn, we all feel the chill of clearer skies and cooler nights. Do not be put off by these conditions. Fishing can be really good at this time of year as fish feed well. I believe that fish may sense the cooling conditions and this triggers a good feeding period as they prepare for winter.

A beautiful, olive-coloured catfish.

Good friends and good catfishing: in beautiful, quiet surroundings a double-figure catfish each for Keith Lambert and Simon Clarke.

One of the great pleasures in recent years has been getting my brother Tim back into fishing more; on our trip to Pitsford Fisheries he caught this lovely 16-pounder. I blanked and didn't mind a bit.

A nice brace of doubles caught in my local Badshot Lea fishery. During the season I caught these fish and many others. I had managed to work out their feeding patterns and was able to catch these two in less than three hours of fishing. I was in bed by midnight, as I was travelling abroad the next day.

A great mate and ultimate handyman Graham Lawrence with a twenty from Yateley.

Ken Latchford with a super 30-pounder from the CCG's Adams Pool fishery.

A rare sight: catfish in the snow. In Spain, catfish have been caught in every month of the year.

Autumn weather in Britain in recent years has been better and better. I cannot remember the last time we had a significant frost before November. It is normally the first really hard frosts that put the fish down and signal the end of the main catfishing season. Fisheries in the south will continue to fish a little later, particularly if, after frost, November is mild. The type of water is also an important factor in determining when catfish slow down. For example, in commercial fisheries with the highest fish stocks, anglers' bait is a significantly greater percentage of the fishes' diet than it is in lower-stocked gravel pits. Such availability of food means that on the commercial fisheries, catfish are typically caught further into cooler weather.

Winter Lottery

Feeding effectively stops after the first few heavy frosts. There are short feeding spells in winter, but they are so infrequent that it makes fishing pretty hopeless. However, it is still worth watching the weather during winter as often there are mild spells in December or January during which a few catfish are caught, usually, I suspect, when the baits land right on their noses.

Many people ask whether catfish do feed in the winter and it is just as it was when carp used to be viewed as uncatchable in winter. In response I would say that there are many waters across the country that contain catfish and carp in which carp anglers regularly catch catfish during spring, summer and autumn; those lakes are also still well fished in winter but catfish captures are virtually unknown in the cold months. Once winter is really established catfish will shut up shop. The same situation also occurs at the end of autumn as the water cools, the fish slow down and feed less.

3 BAITS

As predatory scavengers, catfish have a broad diet and you have a chance of catching one by using almost any bait; however, certain baits have proved more successful than others. Your selection will dictate the rigs and methods that you use.

Natural Baits

Worms
Worms are probably the best natural bait for catfish; unfortunately they are also enjoyed by all other species, so you may well find that the use of worms attracts more attention from 'nuisance' fish than does any other bait. I generally use lobworms, as many as I can fit on to a size 1 hook. Dendrobena worms are also worth using as they are active. If you find you are getting unwelcome attention from other species (tench and perch are the most likely culprits) you can try using worms only after dark. This generally avoids the perch problem but still can result in takes from tench and carp. Fishing a pop-up rig to get the worms off the bottom may also help.

You can freeline or leger worms or use a pop-up rig. Pop-up rigs offer the advantage that the worms are less likely to bury themselves in the

The sun setting means the catfish are coming out to feed. In most lakes they are more confident at night and your chance of a take is better.

lake bottom, and their wriggling attracts catfish. It is also best if the lake has a 'sour' bottom; you can detect a stale smell on retrieving a bottom-fished bait. *See* Chapter 7 for more details.

Worms are a particularly good cool-water bait. If I am fishing on a new water for the first time (particularly if it has been lightly fished) one of my rods will always start with worms. If I receive unwelcome attention from other fish species, I then switch to other baits.

Mussels

Freshwater mussels can make good baits, again subject to hassle from pest species such as tench and carp. You can only experiment on each water and judge which baits to use and how many nuisance fish you encounter. Mussels have always been a successful bait at the famous Claydon lakes, where they can be found in good numbers.

Leeches

These are a deadly bait and the one with which you can be almost totally sure that, when you get a take, it will be a catfish since they do not seem to attract takes from other species. It is sometimes a bait that can trigger a high number of takes, though they seem more effective in some waters than they are in others. The first time they were used at Claydon lakes an angler caught ten catfish in one afternoon, and no other anglers on the lake had a run. The medicinal leech is the usual species used, both here and on the Continent. They can be bought from Biopharm, who have been supplying leeches since 1812 (*see* Appendix II). These leeches are primarily bred for medical use as they are still used by hospitals to assist in ensuring that grafts take and for accidents causing the loss of body parts. Hungry leeches are positioned and, as the leech fastens on, it releases a powerful anti-coagulant. Despite medical advances, the humble leech is still the most effective tool for providing anti-coagulants for this purpose.

Leeches supplied for anglers are the older, larger ones – up to 3in long when contracted and up to 5in when extended. Horse leeches found in Britain may also be used by anglers.

Leeches have a unique, observable, snake-like swimming action. I am convinced that this action is what proves such a good draw to catfish. You have to be careful about the presentation of leeches to minimize their potential for tangling the rig or latching on to the rig and either levering themselves off or at least not swimming. Check out Chapter 7 for details of leech rigs.

If you do obtain some leeches remember that careful storage is essential to ensure that they stay healthy. They should be kept in a refrigerator, preferably in plastic pots with tight lids to prevent their escape. Keep them either in still mineral water or in rain or pond water, but avoid tap water. Split the leeches up so that there are no more than two per pot. This is necessary because leeches release chemicals when they die that can kill other leeches kept with them. Leeches are expensive so careful husbandry is strongly advised.

Crayfish

Crayfish are something of an enigma for catfish anglers. In any catfish water where crayfish are also present it is obvious that the fish feed on them as a staple food source. Frequently you will see catfish pass crayfish claw and bits. However, neither I nor any catfish angler I know has been able to get catfish takes from crayfish, whether used live or dead and despite extensive experimentation with live and dead baits and with various rigs in singles or multiples. I believe that this is a bait that may well benefit from further experimentation and work. Foreign crayfish species, which you are likely to encounter, have proved to be a menace in British stillwaters and rivers. To me, the foreign crayfish is a prime example of a real nuisance alien species that has caused huge damage. Compare this with wels catfish which, by comparison, are not invasive by any interpretation. In several waters, catfish have shown that they can exercise a level of control over crayfish populations, which is something clubs who have crayfish problems may wish to consider. Crayfish should never be moved from water to water.

Maggots

I would not recommend the use of maggots as a hook bait for catfish, but they can be an effective loose feed for attracting them. By putting in good quantities of maggots, up to a gallon over a period of 24 hours, you can attract large numbers of small fish and then the catfish will follow them into that area. You can then position your catfish baits on and near the baited area. This method, fished in conjunction with loose-fed pellets, resulted in my biggest ever catch recently: six catfish totalling 192lb in 13 hours, five of which came in a six-hour period during the late morning and afternoon. All the catfish were caught on lobworms and livebaits, but I am sure that the heavy loose feed contributed to the number of fish visiting my swim.

Livebaits

Catfish are predatory scavengers and, although they will go for an easy food source, livebaiting is an excellent method and it is very rarely that I would not be using at least one livebait. You are not often able to choose what livebaits to use, unless it is at a fishery with many bait fish

Livebait nets are compact, work well and are very handy.

The reason for some missed runs: sometimes catfish (particularly smaller cats) grab baits and run off. Always check baits carefully for teeth marks if you have missed a take.

Fish sections will often sort out bigger cats.

that are easy to catch, but I believe that on most occasions positioning and presentation are more critical factors than the livebait species. As with any fishing, sometimes one method or one livebait species will seem to be the most effective, and researching and understanding such factors are part of watercraft.

You can use a wide variety of size of baits, from 2 to 12oz, though you will need to choose a rig that is suitable for controlling large baits. If you can catch only small livebaits then it is feasible to fish more than one on the hook – two, or even three at a pinch. The catfish mouth is large in relation to the fish's overall size, so even catfish of modest size are able to take large baits.

Livebaits have the advantage of being effective in open water as well as when fished near to features, so having one livebait out can help to spread your baits across your swim to cover the water you can reach effectively. There are a wide

variety of rigs and methods for fishing livebaits – *see* Chapter 7 for details.

The best livebait species are perch, rudd, crucian carp, tench, and roach. Others are small carp, skimmer bream, eels, and gudgeon.

Deadbaits

Deadbaits should be part of any catfish angler's armoury, but they have been widely underused.

Fish

As catfish have such a sensitive sense of smell, a fresh dead fish is highly attractive to them and they will be able to detect it from a considerable distance. I always prefer to catch a fish and kill it (to use it as fresh as possible) though some of the blast-frozen species (eel and lamprey) available through your local tackle shop will also catch.

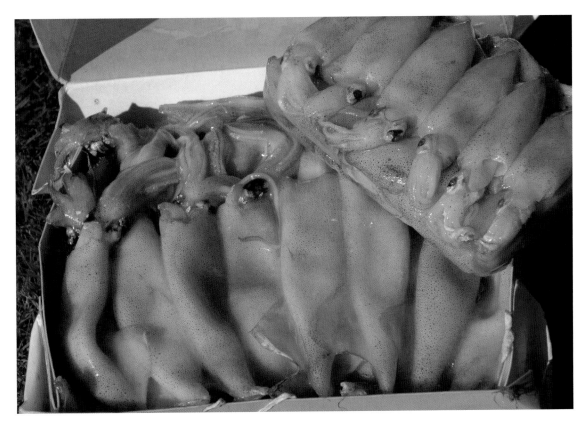

Calamari squid make a brilliant hook bait.

The best freshwater deadbaits are roach, perch, rudd, salmon section, eel sections, lamprey sections, and pike sections (these and lamprey sections are also attractive to pike, so beware – my personal best pike came on a pike section). Other baits worth a try are bream, small carp, crucian carp, tench, and any other freshwater deadbaits. The best sea deadbaits, normally fished in sections, heads or chunks (although any are worth trying), are sprats, sardines and mackerel. (The last is a bait that seems to vary greatly in effectiveness; it has proved useful on several heavily fished waters where the catfish have seen many other baits but much less so on more lightly fished waters.)

Squid and Shellfish

Squid has proved over a great many waters to be a key bait in the catfish angler's armoury.

The best value is the boxed, frozen calamari squid available from tackle shops, or it may be ordered through fishmongers.

Squid can be fished in a number of ways. The calamari squid is usually about 6–8in long and may be used whole, or the head may be removed and the residual body used, or it may be used in small pieces. Whole squid may be freelined or legered, and the body may be used on a pop-up rig, which has worked well for me. See Chapter 7 for a rig diagram.

A particularly effective technique on some waters has been to use very small pieces, as small as 1½in square, in conjunction with trout and halibut pellet loose feed. Building up a bed of pellet, and using small baits, often popped up, has resulted in some good catches. A water where much carp angling takes place is the type of place where this pellet and squid method has

---

Fish Deadbait Preparation

You can use deadbaits whole or just cut the head off a small bait. Bigger baits can be fished as sections (eel or lamprey, for instance). With both types of bait you can also stab them to help the release of smell. I do not think fish oils are needed for catfishing due to the highly developed sense of smell of the wels. Deadbaits can be put on the hook direct or you can use a short hair if you prefer. With directly hooked baits, try to just lightly hook the baits in a firm area so that you can cast them properly, but so that you can also pull the hook out on a strike. For directly hooked baits I would also recommend the use of bait-shields, which help to reduce the risk of the hook's turning and hooking back into the bait when striking.

---

scored. Squid is probably my third favourite catfish bait after worms and livebaits. Other similar baits such as cuttlefish or octopus should work, but I have not tried them myself.

Shellfish baits have also caught catfish, but they are often attractive to carp too and so may be difficult to use to target catfish. Cockles, sea mussels and whelks have all caught catfish and may be worth a try, particularly on well-fished catfish waters. With shellfish, bait presentation can be fiddly because they are soft and susceptible to be pecked off over time by smaller fish; but they may be worth persevering with.

Chicks

Chicks can be bought frozen from pet shops and from companies selling them to use as feed for hawks and reptiles. They have proved to be an effective catfish bait, particularly when prebaited. They have the advantage that they are not attractive to many other species (apart from pike, which can develop a taste for them). To prepare them for prebaiting, chop them up and remove the fluff to prevent them from floating. As a hook bait, remove the head and some fluff and anchor them down with a swan shot or two on the hooklink, 3 or 4in from the hook. Fishing

them close to reeds and cover can work well, particularly when there are ducklings and other water bird chicks around and the catfish may be hunting them or scavenging on fatalities.

Mice and Rats

These have occasionally been used and they may also be bought through pet supplies outlets. A few people have used mice and had the occasional catfish, so they may be worth a try as a novelty; and, of course, mice come with their own hair (the tail).

Static Baits

These exclude fish and other natural baits.

Liver

Liver is underrated as a bait but is well worth using. It has often proved the downfall of some of the biggest fish. It is a soft, bloody bait, cheap to buy and easy to use. You can use almost any type, but chicken, lamb, pig and ox are the main ones. All of these readily leach blood into the water over a period of hours and have accounted for many cats. It is a good bait for prebaiting since it is not taken by many other species (though tench and carp can occasionally be nuisances). Additionally, like squid, if the liver is uneaten and starts to go off, it does not lie on the bottom but floats and will drift away, which ensures that it does not turn the swim off. You can then also check, if you are prebaiting, whether the liver is being eaten. Liver goes relatively quickly from its characteristic bloody purple colour to a pale, creamy brown. Do not be put off by the colour change – liver that has been out for many hours will still get taken.

Other Offal

Kidneys, hearts and other potential baits with a high blood content are good for releasing scent into the water. They are particularly useful on hard-fished waters, where a different bait may score, and on waters with low catfish stocks where they will help to attract fish to the swim.

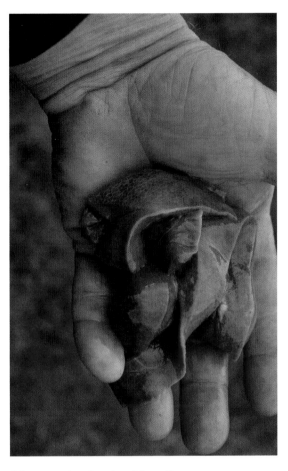

I have caught a lot of catfish on liver.

Don't be afraid of using large meat baits.

Meat

Meats such as luncheon meat, sausage and Spam have proved to be very consistent catfish baits that are particularly effective in the cooler waters of spring and autumn. I think the soft, easily digested nature of meat baits makes them particularly palatable to catfish when, in these cool conditions, their rates of digestion are slower.

Luncheon meat and its varieties do still work well during the summer. However, as they usually also prove attractive to other species of fish, large baits are recommended. For example, to cut a small tin of luncheon meat into three equally sized portions would be ideal on most waters. Meat product baits prepared with skins can also be useful for resisting the attention of other fish. Meat baits can be fished on the hook, but are normally better fished on a hair. *See* Chapter 7 for rig diagrams.

Pastes

Pastes make it possible to combine ingredients and flavours yet still offer catfish a soft, palatable bait, which they prefer to hard baits. With paste it is easy to alter the bait size and consistency. I caught my first ever catfish (in 1985) with a liquidized liver and ground trout pellet paste.

To make up pastes, a coffee grinder and a blender will open up a variety of possibilities. I would recommend that you stick to meat- and fish-based recipes. You can use boilie base mix ingredients and ground pellets as a dry base with a wet additive. I would not recommend the extensive use of artificial flavours because of the sensitivity of the catfish's sense of smell. Pastes receive less attention than they should, particularly on waters where many boilies and pellets are put in, so give them a try.

Boilies

The use of boilies for catfish is a subject that causes much discussion. Many catfish across the country are caught on boilies, but the question is: are they caught because of the boilie or despite the boilie? I believe that catfish do not like boilies – they are hard, and thus they are not as palatable as other baits and cannot be easily digested. The boiled nature of the baits means that the smell release is more limited than from softer baits (such as the same bait mix but prepared as a paste).

However, carp boilies are usually made from good-quality ingredients and flavours, and so, despite their texture and limited flavour release, they do offer the catfish a food source. Where

anglers on a water are targeting carp, there is likely to be, alongside bait, a large bed of free offerings, providing an attractive, easy meal for catfish. If you then multiply this by the number of carp anglers on most waters that also contain catfish, you end with a huge amount of good-quality bait, often in areas where catfish as well as carp shelter or patrol, and it does not take many catfish to stop for a mouthful to result in a good number of them being caught. If boilies are fished over a bed of pellets the attraction becomes greater to catfish, with the fish oils that the pellets release drawing in fish.

The combination of the large number of anglers fishing boilies and the quality of the bait, despite its hard nature, does mean that many catfish are caught on them. But if you look more objectively at the number of rod hours per take with the use of boilies, the bait suddenly looks a lot less effective. As an example, I fished on a 'catfish challenge' at Lakemore Fisheries. The fishery has a reputation for catfish being caught on boilies (and halibut pellets), and since

There are a huge variety of flavours on the market – stick to natural ones.

*Catfish-Pro Moggie
Chunks are softer and far
more palatable to catfish
than boilies or pellets.*

it is also a carp fishery most people use boilies or pellets.

During the challenge there were about 36 rods out for catfish, and I estimate that more than half had pellets or boilies on. There were eight catfish caught, one on a pellet and the rest on catfish methods (fish and worms). I would confidently state that catfish methods and baits will out-fish boilies and pellets probably 90 per cent of the time.

Anglers using 'the method' seem to have a high hit rate from catfish, compared with that achieved when boilies are fished on the straight-forward leger rigs. (Method fishing is using an in-line feeder on which you mould groundbait to offer the fish a soft bait bed next to your hook bait.) So it may be the method, rather than the bait, that increases the likelihood of a take. Why might this be? Catfish are inquisitive creatures and the sound of regular casting and a bed of soft ingredients, with many other fish milling around, often proves irresistible. When catfish respond to the method I do not think they are coming to attack the small fish likely to be present; rather they are attracted by the noise, general activity and food smell.

Observing other anglers and speaking to fishery owners will often enable you to pick up snippets of information like this, though you should always balance them with your own views.

Which Boilie?

There are many varieties of boilies and flavours, so if you are planning to catch catfish on boilies which do you use? Think about the catfish's natural diet first. Fishmeal bases are an obvious starting point with meat or fish flavours. Of the ready-made varieties, of all the captures I hear about, Activ-8-based boilies seem to produce catfish more consistently than any others, though this is an impression as opposed to a finding based on research.

Larger than usual boilies can also help to target catfish specifically and to avoid the attention of smaller fish, such as small carp, bream and tench, increasing the chances of the take being a catfish. A boilie of 25–35mm would normally be large enough to avoid other species, though even larger ones have been used. Instead of very large, individual baits you can achieve the same result by fishing multiple baits on a hair. I have heard of people using baits of up to 70mm, but I see no

The high oil content of halibut pellets has proved attractive to catfish where there is competition for food and substantial quantities are put in.

need to use baits of anywhere near that size in Britain. Boilies should be hair-rigged to ensure the maximum hook-up rate, the bare hook having a better chance of getting a hook hold.

If you are making your own boilies, I would recommend that you do not make them too hard. A softer bait that breaks down more quickly will be considerably more attractive to catfish than one that sits intact for days, not releasing smell. Hard baits are likely to be taken only when a catfish is mopping up a bed of bait: they are not in themselves attractive enough to be targeted individually.

Boilie Pellets

Some boilie pellets are now available. These are softer than traditional boilies and usually cylindrical in shape, and they can be fished over a bed of baits such as pellets. Compared with traditional boilies, the softer texture and faster breakdown of boilie pellets are more attractive to catfish, have a more effective smell release, and are likely to result in better catch rates. The Catfish-Pro Moggie Chunks have proved effective on a number of waters. They have a shorter breakdown period than boilies have, but you

can nevertheless fish them for up to 24 hours and, since the breakdown is gradual, the smell is continually released to ensure that your bait remains attractive.

Pellets

The increased use of pellets, as well as boilies, has made a significant difference to the weights of many species of fish across the country. There are now more waters than ever before containing large carp, bream, tench and catfish. All fish living in lakes visited by anglers have a significant proportion of their diet made up of anglers' baits. The growth in carp fishing in particular has resulted in greater quantities of good-quality bait being thrown in, resulting in the fish attaining bigger and bigger sizes. This has occurred in both newer commercial fisheries as well as traditional club lakes that have not previously seen such significant fish growth. Pellets are, of course, formulated for fish growth so we should not be greatly surprised by this, but it does reinforce the importance of anglers' bait in fish diet.

What do we mean by pellets? There are a great many differently formulated pellets on the market – carp pellets, trout pellets and, most significantly of all, halibut pellets. Halibut pellets have proved very effective for carp and have caught many catfish too.

Kevin Maddocks was the man who popularized halibut pellets when he marketed them as Carp Nuggets. Halibut pellets are rich, with a high fish-oil content; they have slower breakdown rates than trout or carp pellets. The pellets are excellent as a loose feed for catfish and can be effective as a hook bait too. Their smell and oiliness is very attractive to catfish; but they are also quite hard, which makes them less attractive than they otherwise would be. Despite this, the pellets have proved to be very effective in some waters, often those where a lot of carp fishing is done. At certain times they can out-fish traditional catfish methods (such as the use of deadbaits, livebaits and static soft baits); however, I maintain my view that in all but exceptional circumstances traditional methods will catch as many catfish as pellets will. I reiterate the point that, per rod fished, traditional methods will normally out-fish pellet and boilies. Beds of pellets can on occasions get catfish to binge-feed; thus preoccupied, the fish offer the angler the chance of big, multiple catches. So it is a method worth considering, but not worth using exclusively. For loose feed and beds of pellets I make a mixture of pellet types to give a gradual breakdown. Commercial carp pellets will break down quickest, then trout pellets; halibut pellets last the longest owing to their composition and high oil content.

As with boilies, larger baits will often prevent nuisance fish from taking your bait. Halibut pellets are available up to 28mm in size, or multiple 20mm pellets can be fished to form a large hook bait. Hair rigging is essential as pellets cannot be hooked, and large baits impede hook penetration. Halibut pellets must first be drilled before they can be put on a hair; however, they can now be purchased pre-drilled.

The breakdown rates of pellets vary depending on a number of factors – pellet type and size, water temperature, and also the unwanted attention of fish and crayfish. Halibut pellets are usually used as the hook bait, and you can normally expect six to eight hours from a 20–28mm pellet.

Other Baits Worth Trying

Cheese
Cheese-based baits are used extensively in the USA, usually as 'stinky baits' (they have been allowed to decompose before being used). They may be worth trying for catfish but I have not yet done so myself.

Soap
Animal-fat-based soap is used in Africa and has been used in other countries as a catfish bait. As with some baits in Britain, it seems that these soaps are palatable to catfish but to few if any other fish; thus they may be used to ensure that a take is most likely to be from a catfish. It is probably owing to their wide variety of diet that catfish will take these baits more than any other fish species will. Soap baits are not currently available here since they may be subject to import controls because they contain animal products, but it would certainly be an interesting bait to try.

Loose Feed

The term 'loose feed' here refers to free offerings of what is, usually, the bait that is on your hook. The difference between loose feed and beds of bait is that with the latter you are aiming to attract fish to an area that you have baited; the former is more appropriate when you are positioning your hook bait in or close to an area where you think catfish will be lying up or patrolling.

I would usually throw in a few free samples when using baits such as liver or squid. I would favour a few free offerings when fishing close to snags, overhanging trees, islands, reeds, or in the margins. The amount of loose feed to use is a calculation based on your judgement of the number of catfish present, the water temperature, any nuisance fish, and any other specific knowledge of the water you may have. In the spring, in cool water, or on a fishery with few fish, I would put very few loose-feed baits out, possibly four or five pieces. In summer, on a prolific water with

---

Table 5 Loose feeding

Benefits

- The spread of smell could attract fish from further away from your baited area.
- Careful loose feeding should not overfeed fish to ensure the best chance of your bait being taken.
- Line baiting can cover a big intercept area.
- Can trigger competitive feeding among fish.
- If nuisance fish are present they can be fed off with freebies, still leaving your hook bait intact.
- The noise of bait going in can attract fish.

Costs

- The more there is for catfish to choose from, the less likely your hook bait will be taken.
- Uneaten bait could deteriorate and turn off the swim.
- Loose feed could attract other, unwanted species to your swim.
- Fish could spook off a baited area in a heavily fished lake.
- Disturbance from the throwing in could spook fish.
- In cooler water, fish may not feed much and so the loose feed will be an unnecessary distraction.

As you can see, there are pros and cons, so experiment and you should find a balance to suit the water and the time of year you are fishing. In general, the warmer the weather the more loose feed it is likely to be worth using.

If you are feeding pellets as loose feed, spice them with something fishy.

many small catfish I would probably put in five times that number. Here you need to judge the benefits and costs of loose feeding.

I have already referred to maggots, pellets and other baits being effective loose feeds for catfish, and that 'method' fishing has proved to be a way of attracting catfish – the combination of the noise of bait being thrown or catapulted in and the smell of loose feed providing the triggers for catfish to respond to.

Beds of Bait

Any loose offerings can be introduced at the start of a session and topped up over a period. When I use loose feed pellets I usually feed a mixture of different sizes to get a gradual breakdown over a period of hours, the smaller pellets breaking down the most quickly. If you are using maggots and are concerned that they may crawl away on the lake then scald them with boiling water to kill them before use.

Maggots and pellets are good for making a bed of bait to fish over and near. By using small pellets in conjunction with maggots you can attract small and medium-sized fish, which will

Hello, what's that down this catfish's throat? Looks like a small catfish.

Yes, it was a small catfish eaten by the bigger fish – you can tell what it smelt like by the expression on my face. Phew!

then attract catfish into the area. Beds of bait are not necessarily put out to give the catfish a meal but to attract them there.

Prebaiting

Prebaiting can be highly effective for catfishing, and yet it is underused. Many waters do not have large catfish populations, with the result that identifying fish location can be an issue. So why not get the fish to come to you? Prebaiting over a period can be used to get fish to visit the same area regularly and to get fish used to a particular, non-natural, bait. Both will increase your chances of catching and put you in control. Prebaiting is time-efficient in that it is easy to treat multiple swims and multiple waters, and is particularly useful if you are short of time. My preferred prebaits are liver, squid, chicks or Moggie Chunks. If pike are not too much of a nuisance, also try chopped fish (sardines or sprats).

I have often discussed fisheries where 'hot swims' are invariably occupied by other anglers; prebaiting is a way of moving the fish to an area that you have better access to. I would also strongly recommend prebaiting a lake if you believe there are catfish present but cannot be sure – both to increase your chance of catching and to see whether the bait you are putting in is being eaten. You can do this in clear water by

positioning bait in a place where you can see the bottom (making sure that it is unlikely to be eaten by birds). If water conditions are murky, you can use squid or liver, since, when these baits go off, they float, enabling you to monitor the area to see whether bait is being eaten. You can then often see an uneaten bait floating in the margins. The floating away of uneaten bait also prevents the swim from becoming unattractive as a result of bait rotting on the bottom.

Prebaiting can also enable you to keep more than one water on the go; by baiting multiple waters you can have more than one ready to fish.

The calculation of how much bait to put in is based on an estimation of:

- The catfish population.
- The presence of other fish species that might also eat your prebait.
- The water temperature.
- Other anglers' bait being put in.
- Where you are in a baiting programme.

To start in the close season is not a bad idea, particularly if you are offering the fish a soft, easily digestible bait, since they are looking for an easy food source that does not cause them to expend too much energy in locating and eating it. Build up the baiting as your confidence grows that catfish are eating your offerings.

4 TACKLE, RIGS AND METHODS

Rods

Catfish fight very hard. When they are played to the bank, they are rarely ready for netting and will run off strongly again. Therefore a rod with a through action is ideal to absorb the energy from the fight. If you use a rod with a tippy action you are likely to find that the rod locks up in that it goes to its full curve. From this point you

The Catfish-Pro persuader rod is specially designed for catfish fishing in Britain – it's built in the UK, too.

cease to control the fish as you cannot increase pressure from the rod; all you can do is pull harder yourself, increasing the chance of a hook pull or of the fish getting to snags.

The number of rings on a rod also has an impact: a carp rod with few rings is not utilizing the full curve and action of the rod; a catfish rod should have many rings on it to mirror the rod's action. You rarely have to cast huge distances when catfishing so there is really no reason to use a rod with few rings.

If you want to use your existing tackle then a 2.5 to 3lb test curve (TC) pike is likely to be adequate, though you will notice the difference with a quality catfish rod. Beware of catfish rods that are just carp rods with a catfish label on, and ensure that the rod is what you need.

A few lakes in Britain now hold catfish over 70lb. If you are fishing these lakes, you may need to go heavier, in which case refer to the tackle section in Chapter 3.

Reels

Stout reels are the order of the day for catfishing, and a bait-runner mechanism is essential for many catfish techniques. You will find that the mechanism on reels varies between manufacturers. I always look for a reel whose bait-runner minimum setting is as smooth and light as possible. If the setting is too light you can always tighten it, but if it is tight on its lightest setting it may not be suitable.

Smooth clutch (drag) mechanisms on reels are also recommended since the ability to handle powerful lunges is essential, and if a clutch is sticky you may snap up or have a hook pull. I use

Tackle should be matched to the water you are fishing. Fishing for catfish in this snaggy lake dictates stout tackle and barbless hooks.

and would always recommend the old faithful Shimano Baitrunner B reels. They have a front drag (always better than rear drag, in my opinion), a stout construction, and a decent line capacity, although the line lay is not great. There are three models and I use the 4500B in this country. If your budget does not run to these there are a number of cheaper models on the market, so take your pick, but make sure that you check their clutch and bait-runner mechanism to ensure they are smooth.

Reel Line

Monofilament
When played, catfish tend to stay deep, and you will often fish your line brushing through obstacles. As catfish always like cover, many will be

hooked in snaggy areas, so the use of stout lines with good abrasion tolerance makes a lot of sense. I steer away from many of the carp lines that advertise a low diameter for the breaking strain and use the more robust versions. Some of the main brands I would be happy to use are Pro-Gold, Big Game, Daiwa Sensor or Maxima, and I am sure there are others that would also be suitable. I use a 15lb breaking strain as a standard, but heavier if I am fishing a lake with many snags or where the catfish are particularly large; in these situations I use 18lb/20lb/22lb. But always remember that balanced tackle is important, so if you are using a light rod, say with a 2.25lb test curve, there is little point in using line heavier than 15lb since you are unlikely to test the line any heavier.

If your chosen lake contains only small catfish, then why not lighten up the tackle a little to enjoy the fight? A 5lb catfish will not be able to give you much of a fight if you are using 20lb line and a 3lb test curve rod; but on a barbel rod with 12lb line the fight is likely to be much more enjoyable.

For all monofilament lines regular replacement is recommended, and keep any spare line in a dark place to maintain it in the best condition.

Braid

As braided line has virtually no stretch, it is common generally to use braided line with a higher breaking strain than that of the monofilament line. For Britain, 25 or 30lb is normal. Most makes on the market are suitable, so get some advice from your local tackle shop on the choices available. If you are fishing a heavily fished water, a specialist sinking braid may be better since the line will then lie hard on the bottom and reduce the chance of spooking catfish in your swim.

Braid has the advantage that it does not break down when exposed to sunlight and can last many years, but always check your line before using it.

Terminal Tackle

This is the business end of your tackle. It is the only part that comes into contact with fish and it is therefore the most critical. Hard-fighting catfish will test every item of your tackle to the limit, so good condition, top-quality terminal tackle is essential to avoid missed takes or lost fish. Catfish are not particularly rig shy, and so upgrading your tackle in strength is not going to cost you takes, but it will increase the proportion of fish hooked being landed. If you are fishing for really big fish, and in snaggy waters, upgrade your tackle to match the conditions.

Hooklinks

The most common cause of catfish being lost when accidentally hooked is the breaking or wearing through of hooklinks. A good-quality catfish hooklink is therefore a vital element of your tackle. There is a big difference between a catfish hooklink and a carp hooklink, which should be remembered when someone tells you, 'You can use that for catfish,' or 'That will do for catfish.' Most carp hooklinks are not up to the

Catlink is a brilliant hooklink for catfish.

job, and skin-type hooklinks are not suitable. I have heard enough tales of lost fish and taken enough snapped-off carp rigs out of catfish to know what I'm talking about.

Catlink is an aramid hooklink, ultra-tough wearing, of narrow diameter and perfect for the job. Trusty old Quicksilver will also serve, though it is rather light on its breaking strain for many of the bigger fish waters.

There are two types of hooklink for two distinct types of fishing: for static bait fishing (everything except livebaiting) braided hooklinks are best as they are limp, and correct hooklinks are tough and can stand up to the catfish's abrasive teeth; catfish feeding on static baits are usually nervous and picky, often dropping baits if they feel increased resistance. For most live-baiting braided hooklinks will tangle; this is owed to the limp nature of braided lines, thus thick monofilament lines are more suitable. The low-memory, stiff monos such as Toughlink, Stiffy or Amnesia, or strong mainline monos are what you need. I mostly use 25lb Toughlink or 22lb Pro-Gold; you can use other monos

I've caught a few other fish by accident when catfishing, and this was the best by far. This is an old female pike that I caught three years in a row – the first time by accident on a smelly, dead roach, the following year by design on a dead chick, and the next time (when this picture was taken) on a section of pike flesh. The three captures were at 25-01, 27-06 and here at 29-07 – a big fish for September. With not too many fish patrolling the margins at night she was rarely caught by the pike anglers.

but I would not recommend anything lighter than 20lb.

If you are fishing a lake with many pike you can usually get away with Catlink, but if you are getting cut off, or if the local rules dictate that livebaits must be fished with wire hooklinks, check out Pikesafe from Catfish-Pro, a soft, knottable PVC-covered wire. For static baits you could also use new-technology, hybrid hooklinks such as KevsteelX, which is a combined wire/aramid hooklink that is pike-proof yet still limp.

Hooks

A very strong hook is essential because many catfish are lost when inadequate hooks straighten during a fight. Look for a catfish pattern such as Eagle Wave, which has all the key design points for a catfish hook:

- Thick-gauge wire for strength.
- Wide gape to accommodate bulky baits and to find a hook hold in the catfish's large mouth.
- Long point to penetrate bulky baits and still maximize hook up.
- Offset point, to maximize hook up in the catfish's flat and largely bony mouth.
- Sharpness.

Once you have determined your hook pattern, make sure that you use a big enough hook. A 10lb catfish has a mouth 4–5in wide: a small hook can be lost and will increase the chance of striking straight out of the fish's mouth.

I am asked more questions about hook sizes than I am about almost any other topic, and my answer is always the same: the hook size you use should be proportional to the size of the bait, so if you are using a large lump of luncheon meat use a 1/0 or a 2/0 hook. Table 6 (*see* right) gives a rough guide. Hooks should always be checked before use to ensure that they are sharp.

Circle Hooks

Circle hooks are becoming popular, particularly for livebaiting. These are unusual in appearance in that they have a circular shape with an inbent point and are designed to flex and grip in a fish's

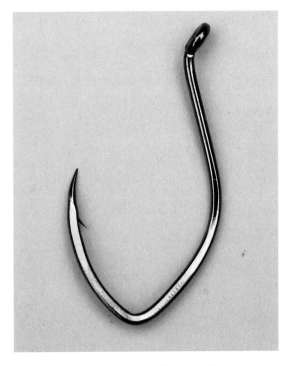

The distinctive Maruto Eagle Wave, simply the best all-round catfish hook.

Table 6 Matching hook size to bait	
Hook size	**Baits**
4	1 or 2 lobworms, other small baits if fishing for smaller cats
2	2–4oz fish, leeches, 15mm pellets, boilies
1	5–6oz fish, lobworms, 20mm pellets or boilies
1/0	7–8oz fish, pastes, meat, squid sections, 28mm pellets, eel section
2/0	9–10oz fish, pastes, big luncheon meat pieces, whole calamari squid

Hook sizes are based on Eagle Wave hooks; adjust the size if you are using smaller patterns.

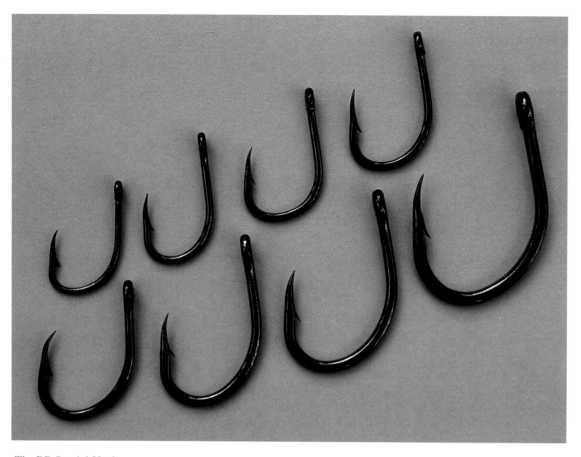

The BP Special Hook.

mouth on a take. They were originally designed for some of the bony-mouth, marine sport fish such as tuna and tarpon; circle hooks have proved useful for catfishing as well. They will normally give you a good hook-up rate, though you have to remember not to strike. When you get a take on a circle hook you just wind into the fish and the hook then flexes and takes a grip, but it can take some getting used to.

Hooks for Boilies and Pellets
If you are fishing smaller, carp-style baits and expect catfish as well, then in the appropriate situation a smaller hook with shorter shank may be suitable. The BP Special Hook pattern from Catfish-Pro is designed for this use. The thick gauge offers insurance in case a big fish is hooked.

Other Key Terminal Tackle

Swivels should be strong. I would recommend 100lb-rated swivels to lessen the risk of failure; to use lighter swivels is pointless.

Ceramic run-rings enable you to make low-resistance leger rings; these are ideal for running leger rigs and for winching baits out.

Bait-shields are dense rubber discs which you can put on your hook after the bait to keep the bait from slipping out; this is particularly necessary for soft baits such as worms and live-baits. Bait-shields can also be used on a hair to prevent soft baits and drilled pellets from falling over an ordinary boilie stop, and if you are using barbless hooks they become essential to prevent bait loss.

Big rubber beads help to reduce the risk of knot damage, particularly when you use heavy leads for longer distance and winching baits out.

Polyballs, foam poppers and deadbait sticks have a wide variety of applications, from making buoyant leger links to popping up baits and making special buoyant catfish rigs.

Any rig that may be taken whole into the catfish's mouth (such as leech and worm rigs and in-line polyball rig) should be equipped with soft poppers which will flatten to reduce the risk of ejection of the hook and maximize the chance of your hook getting a firm grip in the fish's mouth. Clip-on rig rattles can enhance livebait rigs.

Rigs and Methods

The basic methods are divided quite distinctly into three main categories:

1. Static baits.
2. Livebaits.
3. Lure fishing.

Bait-shields are a handy item to keep baits on the hook, particularly for worms and livebaits on barbed hooks; they are vital if you have to use barbless hooks.

Catfish-Pro pro-poppers are soft, foam balls ideal for all buoyant catfish rigs.

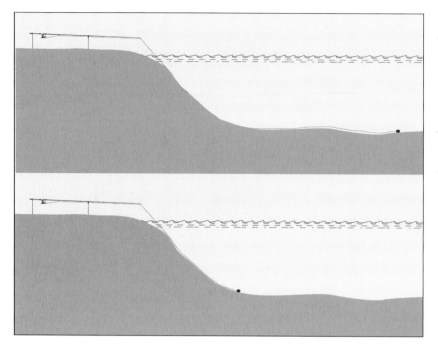

Freeline is always my first choice for static baits, whether fishing in the margins or further out. By leaving the line slack it will rest on the bottom, minimizing the risk of the fish spooking from touching your line. For early bite indication with this set-up, keep your bite alarm on a very sensitive setting to detect any movement.

Static Baits

The simplest – and highly effective – method of catfishing involves the use of static baits (everything except livebaits). With static baits, you are targeting catfish when they are scavenging.

Freelining

Freelining is generally underused; it is ideal for margin fishing for two primary reasons. Firstly, the fish does not feel resistance when it picks up the bait, giving more confident takes and fewer dropped baits. Secondly, the limp line on a freeline minimizes the chance that a catfish will sense or touch your line and spook off the bait.

Freelining suits static baits. When catfish are scavenging they are generally quite careful and will often sample baits and move around baited areas before taking. It is common to get twitches on the line or a single beep on the bite alarm when catfish are around. If you see or hear this get ready because a run often follows. I believe catfish usually swim into a baited area, pick up a bait and then swim off, as opposed to staying on the spot feeding hard. Like other species, they

can, on occasion, become preoccupied and binge feed but this is less common. When freelining I normally fish a 12–18in Catlink hooklink. Catlink is ideal as a sinking, high-abrasion, resistant yet supple hooklink.

Disposable Weight
If you want to freeline but need to cast a reasonable distance, you could use either a heavier bait or a disposable weight. For the latter I use modelling clay, which I make into a ring. I then use PVA string to tie the clay loop to the swivel. The PVA then melts, leaving you freelining. You could use pebbles in a PVA bag as an alternative.

Bite Indication When Freelining
This is a much discussed topic, 'What if the fish swims towards you?' is the question asked most often. I would answer by saying that I generally fish freeline at short range (in the margins most often) and so the range a fish can move in without indication is short. For getting the fastest possible bite indication when you are fishing close to snags, legering may well be a more suitable method.

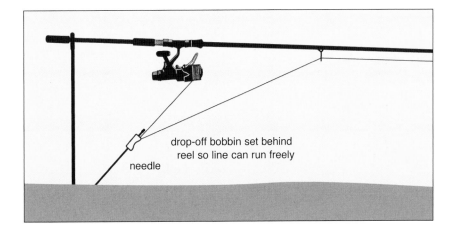

Simple, light, drop-off bobbins are recommended for static bait fishing.

drop-off bobbin set behind
reel so line can run freely

needle

Swingers and Needles

The bite indication set-up at the rod end is just as important as a well-presented freelined bait. Many catfish runs have been dropped through bobbins and swingers offering too much resistance. I do not believe that there is any use for swinger-type bobbins when catfishing: there is resistance, and when catfish feel resistance, or a change of resistance, they are likely to drop the bait. With catfish, the small benefit you might get from a drop-back bite is not worth it.

The best method is an old-style, drop-off bobbin. Position the needle (I use a spoke from an old fishing umbrella), slightly behind the reel and angled towards the butt ring. Use as light a bobbin as you can and position it so that it can drop off the needle smoothly when a take occurs. If you find the bobbin creeps up over time from drag or wind, try putting the rod tip under water or, if this is not possible, squeeze a swan shot or two on to the bobbin to add a little weight.

On very still nights I have even on occasion fished with no bobbin and just opened the bail arm and allowed a couple of loops of line to come off the spool, though conditions are rarely still enough to do this. For freelining I always fish with an open bail arm to allow line to run freely.

Bait-Runners

Catfish, like eels and pike in particular, do not like a change in resistance when taking a bait, so using a reel on a bait-runner/free spool is an alternative. Keep the line to the bait relatively tight; have no bobbin but have the bait-runner on. Always have the bait-runner set to the minimum resistance setting.

Legering

If you cannot accurately position your bait when freelining, and you need to get out further or you are concerned about bite indication, then legering is a suitable method to use. There are a few key points to bear in mind when legering static baits.

First, use a reasonably heavy lead so that, when you get a take, the lead does not move or bump (2oz at close range, up to 3oz at longer ranges are ideal). This is important because bumping or movement could trigger a dropped take. I always recommend fishing any lead in conjunction with a low-resistance run-ring on the lead link. The Catfish-Pro ceramic run-rings are ideal for making into lead links, they are hard wearing and have very low resistance. Second, beware tight lines; slacken your mainline slightly so that you have 10–20yd of line at the business end of your set-up on the bottom. This will mean that you may see the line twitch and lift before you the registration on any alarm or bobbins.

When legering, bobbin set-ups should be the same as for freelining, as I would always recommend running leads. I see no need for fixed or

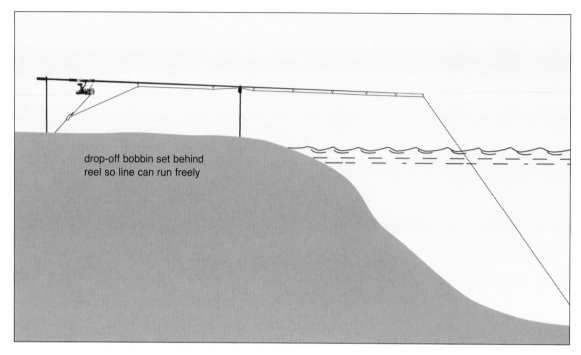

drop-off bobbin set behind
reel so line can run freely

This set-up minimizes dropped runs.

semi-fixed leads when catfishing. With a large mouth and much of it bony, it seems much easier for catfish to drop a hook bait than for carp.

Bolt rigs do not offer any significant benefit and may even cost you the catch if they cause the fish to drop the bait. Some anglers do use bolt rigs when using pellets or boilies, and this would be the only method for which it would make sense.

In many cases, legering involves positioning baits close to areas of cover, so immediate bite indication is important if you are to react in time to move hooked fish away from danger areas.

Legering Rigs
Boilies, pellets and boilie-pellets can all be fished on running leger rigs with bait hair rigged. Make sure you use a large enough hook, particularly when using large or multiple baits. The catfish's mouth is huge, and with small hooks a strike can easily pull the bait and hook straight out.

Many anglers do use bolt rigs and do catch catfish, but it is more risky than the running leger rig because it relies on the catfish taking the bait confidently so that the bait is well into the mouth. And since catfish will often sample baits before taking them, a bolt rig may well spook them off.

If you are fishing soft, meaty baits (luncheon meat, sausage, paste and worms, for instance) then you can either fish them direct on to the hook or on a hair. If you are hooking the bait direct use a large catfish hook with a long point (the Eagle Wave hook is ideal). Bury the hook fully in the soft bait, or, for worms, put as many as you can on the hook. When you get a take, a firm strike will pull the hook through the soft bait to achieve a good hook hold.

If you are using a hair rig, some tubing on the hair can help to grip on to the bait. Using Catfish-Pro bait-shields ahead of a boilie stop will prevent the bait from sliding off.

Squid, liver and deadbaits may be tricky to hook well and are bulky too, which can often turn and mask the hook point when you strike. For these baits, either nick them lightly through

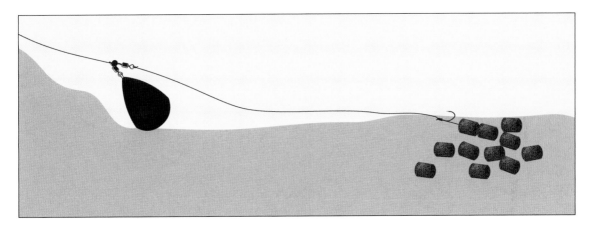

Pellets or boilies can be fished on a standard running leger rig.

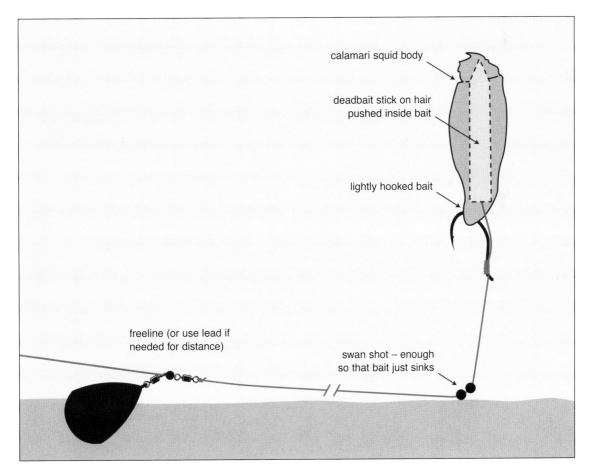

My pop-up squid rig has proved very effective. I use a deadbait stick on a hair and the hook is just nicked through the bottom of the bait.

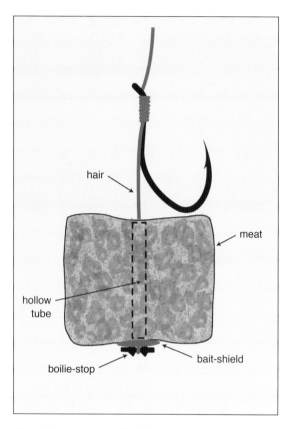

A good way to present luncheon meat.

day catfish may be moving around a lake, not necessarily feeding, and during this activity they will often encounter anglers' lines.

I am convinced that they do not like lines, particularly in well-fished lakes, and if there are many lines in the water, tight ones especially, fish movement is inhibited. I am much more confident on lakes where there are few anglers present, and I am convinced that catch rates are better where there are not many tight lines in the water (such as used on carp rigs). I will always position myself away from other anglers if possible, even when this means fishing a less favoured area. The diagrams opposite graphically demonstrate this; imagine the effect when there are 15 or 20 anglers using tight-line rigs in a small to medium-sized lake.

Livebaits

Legering
Legered livebaits have probably caught more catfish in the country than has any other method. There are many variations to legering and all have their purpose. These variations are designed for specific baits and for positioning the bait at the appropriate depth in the water. All the variations and the rigs are designed to deliver a bait to the 'effective taking zone', that is the area you believe the catfish will be feeding in or that the catfish will be attracted to.

Running Leger
A normal running leger rig will enable you to fish a bait close to the bottom of a lake. This is effective in cooler water conditions when catfish are more sluggish, lying on the bottom for periods of time and will not move far for food. One tip is that if you catch a catfish and it has leeches on it, it will have been lying up for some time. One factor you have to be careful of when using a standard leger rig is the nature and composition of the bottom of the lake: if it is snaggy, there is a risk of your livebait's being buried in weed; and if it is sour with a low oxygen level, you do not want your livebait close to

a firm area of the bait or use a hair rig. As with meaty baits on a hair rig, positioning a bait-shield ahead of a boilie stop will help to stop the bait from sliding off.

Popping this type of bait up off the bottom can prove successful. You can pop the bait up by using a deadbait stick on a hair. By checking the bait in the margins you can adjust the rig buoyancy by adding swan shot to the hooklink to make the rig just sink. By moving the swan shot on the hooklink you can also alter how much you pop the bait up, which is particularly useful if you are fishing over a sour or weedy bottom.

The Impact of Tight Lines
Catfish are highly sensitive and very aware of their environment, hence the need to be quiet on the bank, particularly at night when they are most likely to patrol the margins. At all times of

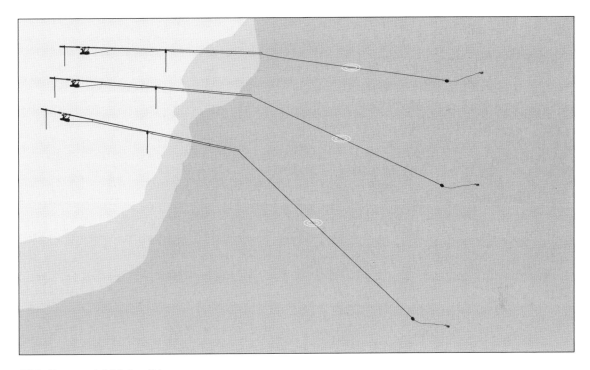

Tight lines can inhibit free fish movement.

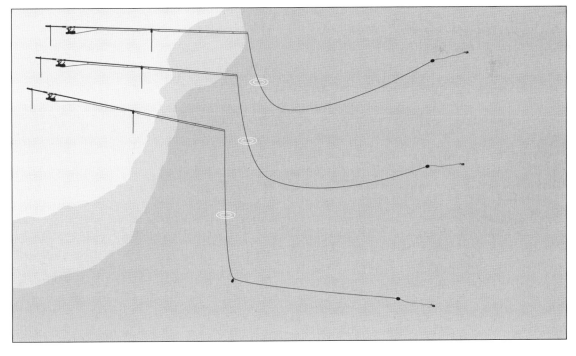

Slack lines reduce fish spooking.

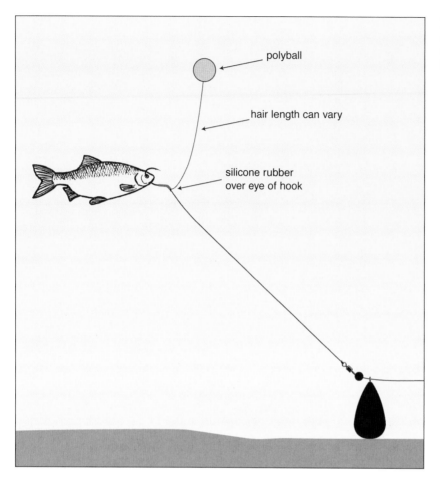

polyball

hair length can vary

silicone rubber
over eye of hook

The polyball rig has accounted for many catfish captures. This is the standard method.

the bottom. This is because the catfish are less likely to be feeding there and less likely to be able to find the bait. This is particularly important if you are using a bait fish species that naturally prefers the bottom, such as crucians or tench. One bait species that is well suited to a running leger rig is rudd; this is because it will almost always try to swim upwards, and so anchoring the bait with a running leger will make it work well.

For all running leger rigs I recommend a good-sized lead (2–3oz), a low-resistance running on the lead link, and monofilament hooklinks. Braided hooklinks are not suitable because livebaits will invariably tangle them up, rendering your rig ineffective. I always fish running leger rigs direct from a bait-runner, without a bobbin.

Catfish will normally take livebaits aggressively and the constant resistance of a lightly set bait-runner will minimize the risk of bait ejection.

The Polyball Rig
The simple addition of a polystyrene ball (polyball) can make a huge difference to a standard running leger in terms of where you can position your bait and how it behaves. It has been an extremely effective rig over many years. Originally popularized by Bob Baldock in the mid-1980s, it has since undergone many adaptations. At its simplest, the polyball rig is a standard running leger fished with a buoyant sphere (commonly a polystyrene ball) on a 6in hair.

The function of the polyball is to raise the livebait in the water: this combats the tendency of

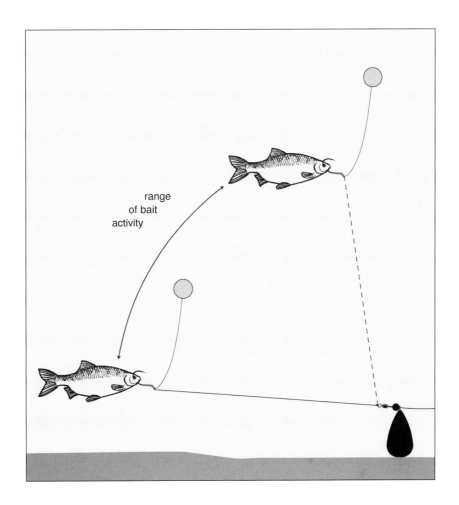

Positioning of polyballed bait. The polyball rig lifts the bait off the bottom and, typically, the bait will then swim downwards in response.

range
of bait
activity

the bait fish to swim to the bottom and increases its activity level. The movement of the bait and the prevention of its hiding on the bottom increase the chances of attracting catfish to take.

POLYBALL OPTIONS

High-density polystyrene balls are best because they cannot be squashed and they are more buoyant than the softer ones. Foam balls such as Catfish-Pro poppers are also recommended. I have previously used Fox poppers but stopped because on several occasions carp have taken them (they are red).

If you are fishing in-line polyballs then foam balls are more suitable than any other because they increase the chance that catfish will take the whole rig when they take the bait; in addition,

foam balls are less likely to impair the hooking of the catfish and cause the fish to reject the bait. Hooking points vary when using polyball rigs and are consistent with leger rigs: the bait is most often nose-hooked, but it is sometimes tail-hooked.

ADJUSTING AND VARYING THE POLYBALL RIG

The size of the polyball will affect the way the bait fish behaves in the water. When considering what size to use, there are three options: first, a large polyball that the bait fish cannot pull down and that will keep the bait high in the water; second, a polyball that the bait fish can pull down, but that will pull the bait fish upwards when the fish is at rest; and third, and least common, a small polyball to prompt the

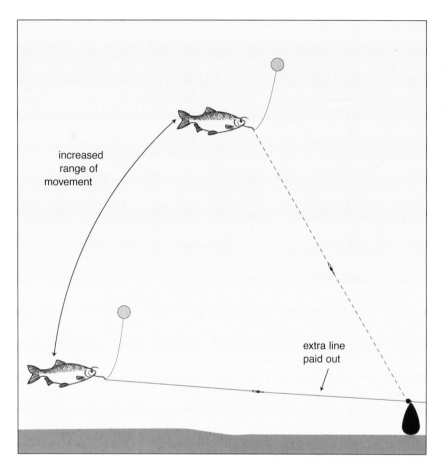

increased
range of
movement

extra line
paid out

*If you pay out the line
on a polyball rig you
can increase the range
of the bait's movement
and allow it to come
up in the water; this is
useful in open water.*

bait fish to move but not buoyant enough to lift a resting fish up.

ROD SET-UP

I fish all polyball rig variations on a running leger with no bobbin but with the line straight off a bait-runner reel. The bait-runner is set at minimum. If you are using large baits, or fishing in flowing water, you may need to tighten the bait-runner (but tighten it gradually so that it is only just tight enough).

PAYING OUT LINE

With a standard polyball rig the area in which the bait moves will be limited by the length of the trace you fish. You can increase the movement range of the bait by paying out more line (*see* diagram above). I would use this method in

open water, normally where there is good depth. This should make for a greater chance that a catfish will intercept the bait. However, I would not pay out extra line if I were fishing near weeds or snags since it would increase the risk of the bait's hiding or, if there is a take, of the catfish's having a better chance of reaching a snag.

The Long-Hair Polyball Rig

One adaptation of the polyball rig that has proved successful for me is the long-hair polyball. With a standard polyball rig you do not know whether your bait is working well. Your bait could be sitting in weed – or even have died – but you would not know because you can only watch the rod tip and the line's twitching, or hold the line in your fingers in

Long-hair method. I tend to use this adapted, long-hair polyball rig because you can dictate the depth at which it fishes and monitor the bait activity by watching the polyball on the surface.

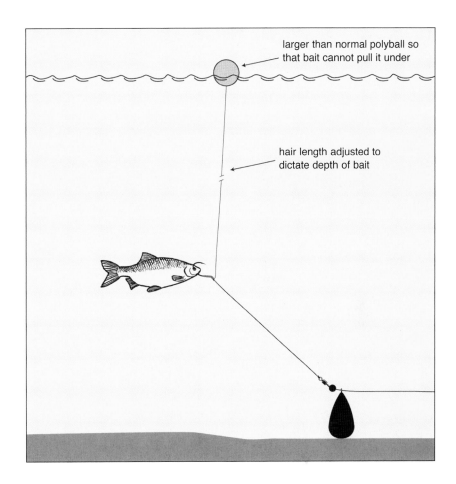

larger than normal polyball so that bait cannot pull it under

hair length adjusted to dictate depth of bait

order to feel whether the bait is tugging. The long-hair polyball rig improves your ability to monitor the bait's activity.

For this method set up your rig with the hair length to match the depth you want to fish the bait at (I have fished with up to 4ft hairs). Use a larger polyball than you normally would so that the bait fish will struggle to pull it under the surface (or succeed in doing so for only a second or two). Then, when you cast or winch your bait out, the polyball will stay on the surface, enabling you to monitor its movement and also to pay out line to allow a greater area for the bait to work in.

A polyball on the surface can also indicate whether the bait is panicking, which would in turn indicate that cats may be in the area. If the polyball goes still for a long period, tug the line

and see whether the bait sets off again; if not, it may be tangled, stuck in weed, or dead.

You can enhance this rig by using Catfish-Pro nightsights. These are polyballs with a swivel in the bottom (to prevent twisting) and a holder in the top into which you can put a starlight, enabling you to monitor your bait at night. This adds to the excitement as, often, you will see the nightsight disappearing, indicating a take, before your alarm registers.

Short-Hair Polyball Rig

This variation on the polyball rig positions the polyball (or soft popper, which is better for this rig). The hair itself has a bait-holding hook, smaller than the main hook, on the end. The exact size of the bait-holding hook is dictated by the size of bait. Separate bait hooks can be used on most livebait rigs facilitating a clear main hook; but beware of local fishery rules since this practice could be interpreted by some as a two-hook rig, which may not be permitted.

In-Line Polyball Rig

This version minimizes tangles and is the only version that works in river conditions. In a river this rig is streamlined and sits in the flow. A standard polyball rig in flowing water normally results in the rig's rotating or the polyball's spinning, leading to tangles.

Instead of positioning the polyball on the hair, slide two foam poppers on to some silicone tubing; slide the tubing down the hooklink and over the eye of the hook to semi-fix it in place. You can also use a rubber float-stop at the other end of the tubing to keep it in place. Use two smaller, soft-foam poppers instead of hard balls, since a confident take on this rig will see the bait, tubing and foam balls all in the catfish's mouth. The soft foam poppers will squash, minimizing bait rejection or the impairing of a hook-up on the strike.

Dumbell Rig

My most consistently successful livebait rig in recent years has been the dumbell. It is a surface rig that enables you to fish your bait in the top 10in of water, critically keeping the area under the bait clear and allowing catfish to strike unimpeded. The anti-tangle nature of the rig also enables you to fish it with a braided hooklink, making bait fish movement more natural.

The dumbell rig is fished as a running leger. Thread your leger link on to the mainline; follow this with a large rubber bead, and then the dumbell. Then tie your swivel on to the mainline and tie on your short hooklink. Once ready, pull the mainline back though the dumbell so that the swivel is pulled into the soft silicone tubing to semi-fix the hooklink. This last step is essential because you need the bait held near the surface. The hooklink needs to be shorter than the length of the dumbell to prevent the bait's being able to swim back and tangle the mainline. When cast in, the buoyancy of the

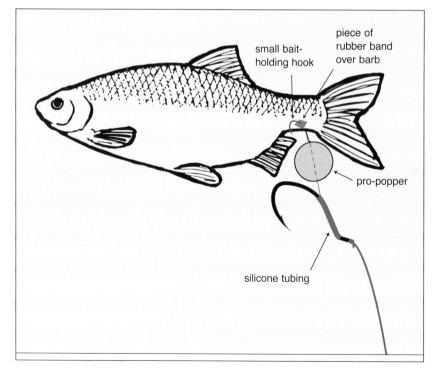

small bait-holding hook

piece of rubber band over barb

pro-popper

silicone tubing

Alternative livebait rig. This short-hair polyball rig is another option suitable for slow-flow river fishing or lakes.

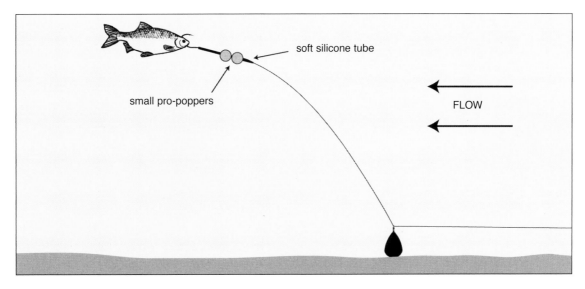

The in-line polyball is one version to use in flowing water to avoid tangles.

dumbell immediately pops it up to the surface. If it does not come up it is likely that the line at the leger link has twisted.

As with the long-hair method of the polyball rig, you can watch the dumbell rig itself when cats come out to monitor the bait fish's movements. You can also increase the area in which the bait can move by paying out line to allow the dumbell to work over a wider area.

Takes on dumbell rigs may be spectacular because they are so close to the surface. Even before the alarm sounds, you often hear the take as the catfish strikes and makes a swirl at the surface. Hooking positions for dumbell rigs are

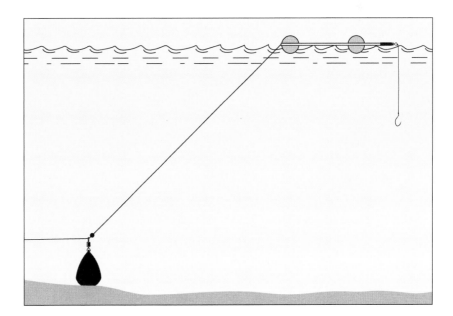

The dumbell rig is a deadly sub-surface one.

A dumbell rig strikes again – a nice 20lb fish.

either through the nose or under the dorsal. I prefer the latter as it enables the livebait to swim away from the rig, which maximizes activity.

As with all livebait rigs, I fish the dumbell set-up with line straight off a bait-runner with no bobbin. The dumbell rig is suitable for water depths to about 10ft; in conditions deeper than

this, paternoster rigs (such as the cat-o-copter) are more suitable.

Submerged Dumbell-Type Rigs
An adapted, submerged version of the dumbell rig has also proved effective when fishing leeches or worms. The leech and worm dumbell rigs are

fished on a running leger, as with a livebait dumbell, but the rigs are much smaller, with smaller poppers. These are designed to be popped up off the bottom. To use this rig, do the following:

1. Set up rig.
2. Bait up and cast in.
3. Carefully tighten down until the hooklink is tight to the lead link.

4. Put the rod in the rod rest and set the bait-runner on.
5. Then – and only then – pull the required amount of line off the bait-runner that you want to pop the bait up by (this way you can be sure how far off the bottom your bait is); you just need to ensure that, when you pay out line, the line is tightening again to show the rig is coming up in the water; leger links with ceramic run-rings can help to ensure this.

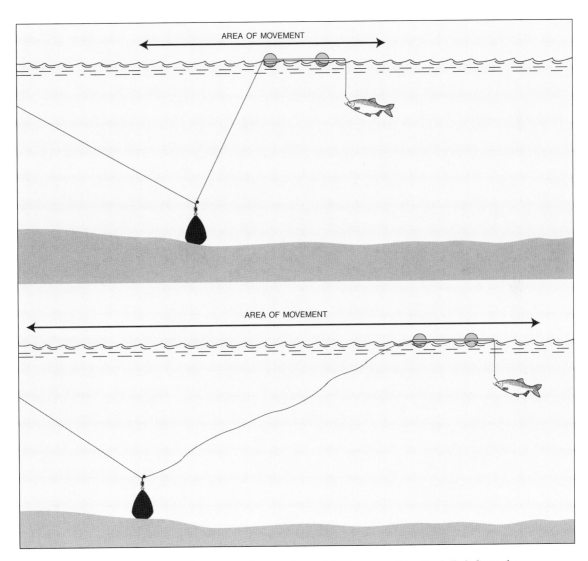

If you pay out line you can cover a larger area of water; the semi-fixed nature of the dumbell rig keeps the livebait close to the surface.

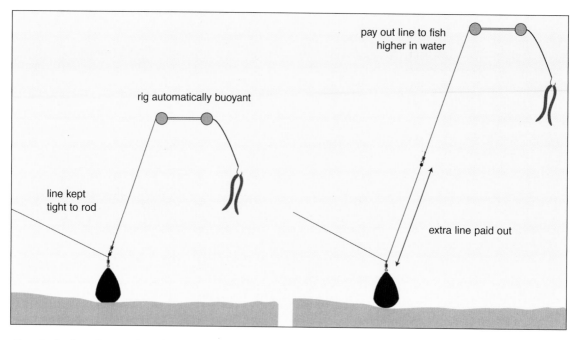

Cast the leech and worm rig, pull rig so it is tight to the swivel, and then pay out the amount of line necessary to allow the rig to lift to the required level in the water.

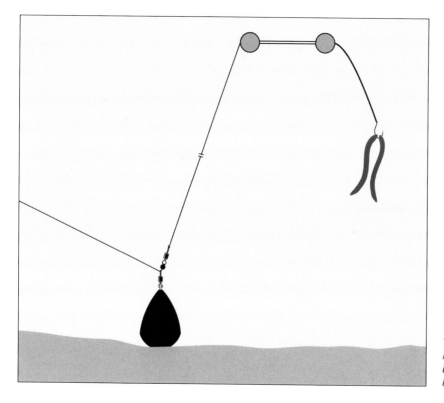

The leech and worm rig keeps the bait off the bottom, preventing the bait from burying itself.

As an alternative to 5: when you cast in, let the rig float up to the surface and then set the rod and pull the line back in to lower it from the surface. Bear in mind, however, that depending on the range and conditions, it may not be easy to see the rig on the surface, and this method is not feasible in the dark.

I would recommend fishing these rigs between 1ft off the bottom and mid-water, although many have had success allowing the bait up to just below or even on the surface.

Rigs are being developed and adapted as more and more catfishing is done. For myself, I do not believe in making rigs too complicated and, as with carp fishing, there can be over development to the detriment of catch rates. However, an adaptation of the submerged dumbell worm rig that I find has worked is the tipper rig (*see diagram below*). This employs the same principle of using a stiff tube and a buoyant ball to suspend a bait above the bottom, with the area below the bait clear of line. The buoyant ball or egg can slide along the rig to balance it against the weight of the bait.

Paternoster Rigs
Paternoster rigs are effective for the main British predator species, including catfish. They enable you to deliver livebaits at a variable

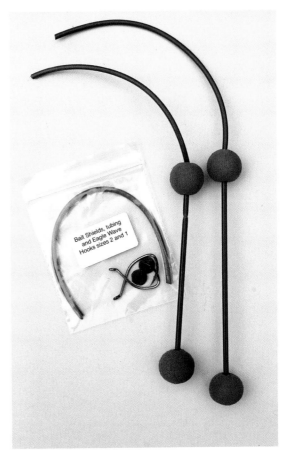

Leech and worm rigs minimize tangles and work well as pop-up rigs.

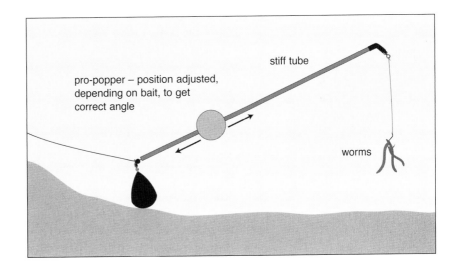

The tipper rig. This adaptation of the dumbell worm rig uses a 12in stiff tube and a movable pro-popper to balance the rig. This is suitable when you want your bait closer to the bottom.

stiff tube

pro-popper – position adjusted, depending on bait, to get correct angle

worms

depth and are rigs which seem to keep livebaits particularly active.

Cat-o-copter Rig

This has proved itself to be effective for catfish; it is a paternoster rig with the simple addition of a second polyball, this one underneath the swivel to which the hooklink is attached. The stop knot at the top of the rig determines the depth the rig is fished at. This additional polyball serves two functions: first, to lift or slide the hooklink and the bait to the desired depth; and, second, to add buoyancy to help keep the rig vertical in the water. As with all paternoster rigs, the hooklink should be kept short, 6–8in, using a stiff hooklink to minimize tangles. The rod is then set up upright in a beachcaster style, with the line under reasonable tension to the rig but without pulling it too far off the vertical. The reel can then be set with a bait-runner. You will usually see the rod top knocking as the bait works and runs are often very fast. If you are fishing over weed beds you can make a long, fixed lead link to ensure that the bait is not caught up. Ensure that you use polyballs or poppers of at least 1.5in diameter because you will not get sufficient buoyancy with smaller ones.

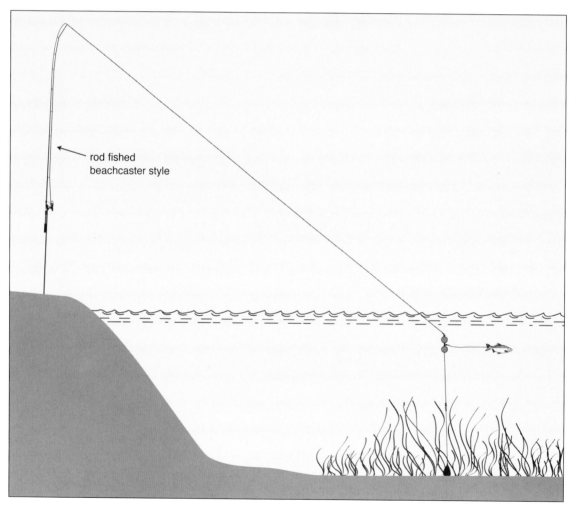

rod fished
beachcaster style

The cat-o-copter is a buoyant paternoster rig; like all paternoster rigs, it tends to keep the bait active.

Float Fishing

A free-roving, float-fished livebait can be very good if you are able to fish the rig effectively: if you can get the bait roving around it can cover a greater area of water than any other livebait method. You can move the bait around to different areas, and the float is a sensitive and immediate indicator of bait panic or a take. For this to work you need plenty of room on a fishery and favourable wind conditions to cause a bait to drift out, as repeated casting tends to affect the bait activity.

Hook Positioning for Livebaits

Hook positions vary depending on the fish and the rig used; you can experiment to see what works best on your water. Most of my livebaits are fished with the hook in the mouth and out through the nostril. A bait-shield put on after the livebait will keep the bait hook secure, especially if you are using barbless hooks.

Legered livebaits with no buoyancy in the rig are often root-hooked at the tail to get them to swim away and increase activity. The hook is usually placed at the bottom of the tail.

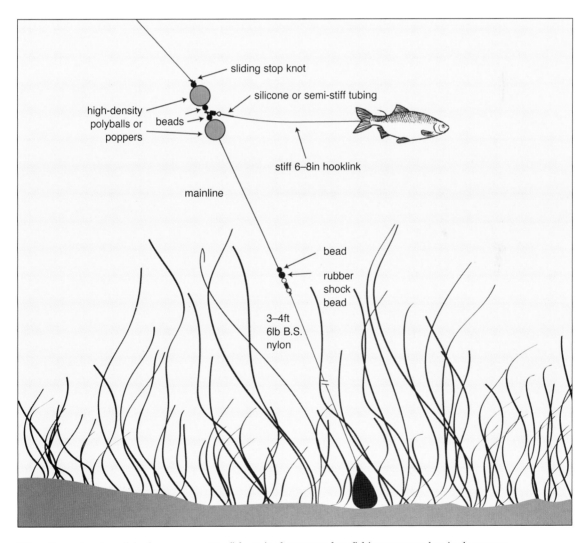

The cat-o-copter is useful when you want to fish up in the water when fishing over weed or in deep water.

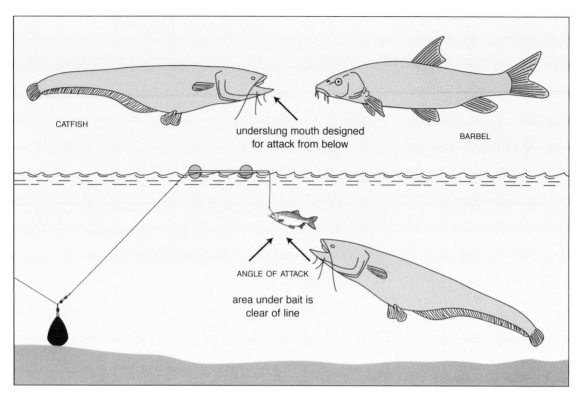

One of the biggest changes in my catfishing has been to fish baits up in the water; when you observe the jaw angle of the catfish it makes sense. Catfish are built to attack from underneath; contrast this with the jaw shape of the bottom-feeding specialist, the barbel.

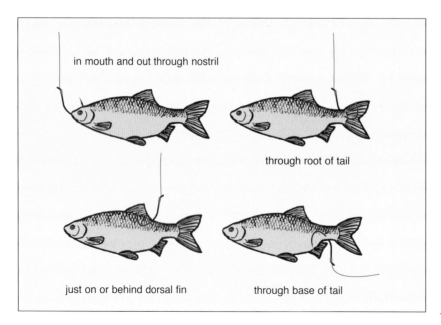

The position of your hook for livebaiting will vary depending on the rig and the bait fish you are using.

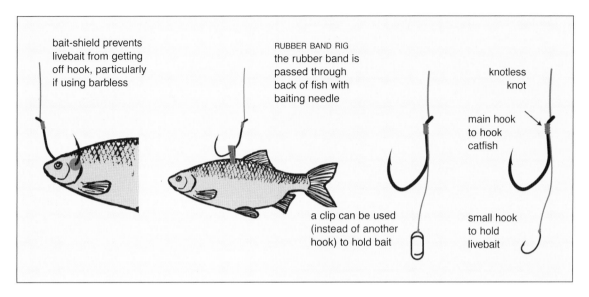

Other hooking arrangements for livebaits.

bait-shield prevents livebait from getting off hook, particularly if using barbless

RUBBER BAND RIG
the rubber band is passed through back of fish with baiting needle

knotless knot

main hook to hook catfish

a clip can be used (instead of another hook) to hold bait

small hook to hold livebait

On dumbell rigs I have usually lip-hooked, but now I am increasingly hooking the bait just behind the dorsal to encourage it to swim away from the rig. You can adapt this arrangement by hooking a small piece of rubber band – passed through the back of the fish with a baiting needle (thus allowing the bait to act more naturally), though care needs to be taken to avoid the bait flying off on the cast. For the cat-o-copter rig I tend to lip-hook or tail-hook baits.

I have also been using hair rigs for livebaits, in some cases with bait clips on a short hair, to enable the fish to move more naturally and to keep the hook clear for striking. This is a handy technique if you are using small baits, and it can also be used for leeches and worms.

Shake, Rattle and Roll

One useful enhancement to pretty much all livebait rigs is the rattle. This is attached to the hooklink: when the rig moves, there is a rattling sound. Rattles perform the dual purposes of keeping your bait active and sending out vibrations that attract catfish. Position the rattles 3–4in from the hook on the hooklink. It has proved particularly effective on float-fishing, dumbell and polyball rigs.

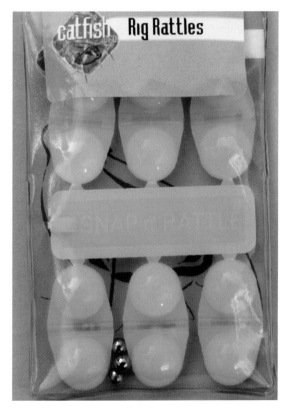

Rig rattles are an effective enhancement to livebait rigs.

But beware: rattles have proved deadly for pike and are also attractive to perch so you may get attention from other fish.

Lure Fishing

Lure fishing is an underused method in Britain, although it could be effective when catfish are in a feeding mood. Unfortunately, the heavily regulated fishing here and the sheer number of anglers make the use of the method limited. Often fisheries have regulations about lure fishing in the summer and the use of treble hooks. These rules are usually set up in good faith to limit pike fishing to the winter, but, unfortunately, they also eliminate lure fishing for catfish. On the waters that I have catfished most in the last two or three years there simply is not enough room to lure fish: most swims are occupied, limiting the amount of open water.

But if you do get an opportunity to try I would recommend the following:

- Traditional spinners, which give off strong vibrations.
- Spoons that have good fish imitation.
- Shads (soft plastic), which can be fished in a jigging style or sink and draw.
- Surface lures, creating disturbance.

There does not seem to be any specific retrieval technique that works with spinners and spoons. My experience with them has been limited, but when it comes to trolling I have been advised that lures can be fished pretty fast to get hits. I assume that this gives the catfish less time to make its mind up.

Bait and Loose-feed Delivery Techniques

Apart from the use of the trusty catapult, there are other techniques with which to deliver bait

There are now some huge catfish in England. Henry Hansen displays this fantastic 85lb specimen.

The biggest fish ever caught in Britain: Chris Wade with a monster 130lb.

and loose feed. Accurate bait positioning and loose feeding are not as important for catfishing as they are for carp fishing, but they can be an advantage on some waters if you want to fish close to features.

If you are using buoyant livebait rigs, such as the polyball or the dumbell, there is always the challenge of getting a good-quality bait out to where you want to fish while keeping it in the best possible condition.

Boats

If you are fortunate – and if the rules allow and the situation is suitable – you can carry or tow baits out with an inflatable boat, though you may disturb the swim. A boat enables you to place baits where you want them and, if fishing static baits, to loose feed directly over them. On weedy lakes it can also enable you to place baits on clear patches. I have a 6ft, inflatable Sevylor boat, which has proved handy on a couple of waters. It can be transported flat, and I have a

A decent inflatable can be invaluable for reconnaissance, baiting up and taking baits out.

fast inflation pump which runs from a 12V car cigarette-lighter socket.

Bait Boats
Again, if the fishery permits and you have one, a bait boat can be useful for catfishing. You can deliver static baits and loose feed effectively, particularly in areas close to cover where casting is risky. For delivering livebaits, all the bait boats I have seen are not great but will do the job. The usual technique is to jam your lead in

the hopper of the boat and tow your bait out. If your bait is large, steering straight may be tricky.

Winching
If boats are not allowed, or you do not have one, a useful technique is to 'winch' your baits out. This is a method of delivering livebaits out to a long distance without having to cast out, giving you the advantage of being able to fish further out than when casting. It enables you to fish with your bait in the best possible condition.

The experienced catfish angler, Bob Warren, with an early-season forty.

STEPS IN WINCHING YOUR BAIT OUT

1. Set up your fishing rod with your usual rig, ideally using a ceramic ring on your lead link, to minimize drag, and using a studded lead instead of the usual 2–3oz, 5–6oz one.
2. Set up a second rod. Use a winch rod or a butt section of an ordinary carp/pike/catfish rod and attach a reel with a 6 or 8lb line to this winch rod; thread the line through the winch rod and then through a buoyant winch body with a snap swivel on the end; put the winch rod into a butt rest just behind you or get someone to hold the winch rod.
3. Connect the two rods by putting the snap swivel at the end of the winch rod on the hook of your main rod, the two rods are now connected and you are ready to use the winch rig.
4. Open the bail on the winch rod and put the line in a clip to prevent the line from falling off. Cast out your rod as far as you want to; the line should flow freely from the winch rod. You should now have your line cast out attached to the winch rod line.
5. The buoyant winch body should come up to the surface.
6. Now put your main rod on a rod rest (with open bail arm) and pick up the winch rod;

Kevin Midmore, with a nice Woburn Abbey catfish – a direct descendant of the fish that were stocked some 120 years ago.

Pete Shefford with a lovely 55-pounder from Great Linford Lakes.

reel in the line on the winch rod slowly and carefully (the lead you have cast out should stay put with the line being pulled off the main rod); continue to reel in until the winch buoyant body reaches the bank.

7. Unclip the end of the main rod line and attach your rig to it.

8. Put your baited rig into the margins and then pick up your main rod and wind your line; your rig should then be pulled out into the lake and will stop only when the rig reaches the end of your mainline.

Problems to watch out for and how to solve them:

1. You cast out your main rod, but the drag from the winch-rod line shortens your cast too much.

   To solve: use a bigger lead/cast harder to allow for extra drag. Check your reel on the second rod to ensure that the spool is well filled and can flow freely.

2. You cast out the main rod, and the line from the second rod crosses over the mainline, shortening the cast.

   To solve: always have the winch rod downwind of the main rod.

3. When you start to wind in the winch rod, the line does not come off the reel on the main rod.

Cameraman James Hargreaves filming at Red Beeches during the shoot of A Catfishing Season; *Richard Garner had landed this lovely fish, the biggest ever caught from this water.*

To solve: the lead is moving (which it should not do), or it is tangled. Reel in both rods and try again; if the problem persists use bigger lead. Note: braided mainline is usually better than mono for winching.

4. People look at you strangely.

To solve: say nothing and catch more fish; people will stop looking at you strangely and will start being friendly to find out what you are doing that is working so well.

Winching is difficult to explain in text or drawings. The easiest way to understand it is to watch someone else or see it being clearly demonstrated on the DVD *A Catfishing Season*, available from the CCG.

5 CATFISH ACTION!

Now that you have an idea of the baits, rigs and methods, you can choose your set-up to suit the fishery you are visiting.

Match Your Set-Up to the Situation

Catfish are pound for pound the hardest fighting fish in the United Kingdom, so if you are targeting them you need to be prepared; and if you're

Heave! There's a big catfish on the end, about 150 yards away.

fishing for other species you need to be careful as they might take your bait.

How big do they grow and what type of fishery and swim are you fishing? Set up your tackle to to take account of these factors. If it is an open lake with no snags, and the catfish grow to only about 20lb, then you will have time to play the fish and the risk of losing them is relatively low. However, with all catfish – even in this environment – the two most important points are:

1. To use the appropriate hook.
   All catfish have large mouths and abrasive teeth – and they fight hard – so you should use larger than usual hooks. Use a catfish pattern (to reduce the risk of the hook's straightening), and a proper catfish hooklink to eliminate the risk of its wearing through. Hooks should match the type and size of your bait. Other than when float fishing for kittens, I have never used a hook smaller than a size 2 for catfishing; I usually use a 1 or a 1/0.
2. To use the right hooklink.
   The great majority of catfish losses are owed to hook pulls or the wearing through of hooklinks. A true catfish hooklink such as Catlink is ideal and far more suitable than a carp hooklink (which is not designed to stand up to the catfish's abrasive teeth).

Some fisheries specify the use of barbless hooks, so that in the unfortunate event of losing a fish the hook will be ejected easily. Even if the fishery does not demand it, consider using barbless hooks to ensure that a lost fish will not be damaged by a rig's trailing from it.

If you are fishing in a snaggy lake then uprate your tackle to enable you to keep a fish away

There is nothing harder than trying to catch catfish for the camera. On the first shoot for the DVD A Catfishing Season, *we fished at Pitsford in April. It was bitterly cold, but I managed to catch three doubles, which was a great result.*

from snags if possible. Mentally plan in advance how you are going to react when you get a take in a snaggy area. How will you keep the fish out of the snag? A quick strike and immediate pressure can turn a fish before it gets up a head of steam, and heavier line can give you a real advantage; on some lakes I even use a heavy shockleader to give me extra protection from underwater obstacles. Some fish in snaggy lakes are aware of refuges and will head there when hooked, so try to out-think them.

Catfish will normally hug the bottom and fight for a long time, so be prepared for a long battle and do not become too anxious. Set your clutch carefully and bear in mind that, when the catfish comes to the bank, it may not be ready to net. Often the fight is only starting when it comes near the net.

From what you know and can learn about the water, select your rigs and baits, cast out, and you are in business.

Catfish Takes

Bites or takes from catfish are normally quite violent. They are often shy and sensitive when out on the feed, but when they take the bait

Nearly there – a tired catfish is almost ready to land.

things become fierce. There is normally a grab, then a split-second delay, followed by a screaming run. Anglers often ask me when to hit runs and my advice is that you should get to your rod and strike fairly quickly but not in a panic. Always take time to get your bearings. Wind down hard and strike to set the hook. Then the fun can really start.

Catfish will normally run hard and almost always stay deep for most of the fight. In shallow water you may get a slap of the tail at the start of a fight. Stay calm when playing cats, and keep everything smooth. You may experience odd bangs on the rod followed by a moment's slack line (as if you had lost the fish). This is caused by the catfish's tail whipping round and striking the line; after the tail strike you get the moment of slackness.

Catfish do not usually head for snags (as carp would), but you do sometimes encounter some wise fish that do not follow the rules. As the catfish starts to tire it will come up to the surface, but this is the time to take particular care. As the fish gets close I always slightly loosen the clutch to accommodate late dives on a short line.

Landing Catfish

Now the catfish is played out how are you going to land it? Catfish are very long for their weight and can swim backwards. A 50lb fish can easily be 5ft long, so getting the fish into the landing net can be tricky. If you are lucky, the fish will curl into a horseshoe shape if you slightly relax the line when the fish is over the net, but often a small amount of the tail over the drawstring will result in the fish's slipping out backwards.

A handy piece of tackle is the Catfish-Pro catfish landing net, with 60 or 72in arms and 4ft deep mesh. This saves your having to scoop at a fish; you can leave the net in position and draw the fish over it.

Gloving

If you are really caught out with an inadequate net and a very big fish you may have to try to beach the fish (which is very tricky) or hand-land it. Hand-landing is the standard method for fishing abroad but it can also be used in Britain if needed. To hand-land it is best to use a soft glove. On the Continent, gaffs are sometimes used, but there should be no need to use one on a catfish: gloves should be sufficient to land any fish.

When hand-landing a catfish, the first thing is to check where the hook is in the fish's mouth to ensure there is only the smallest chance of the hook's ending up in your hand. Secondly – and this is very important – tap the catfish on the top of the head to determine whether it is ready to

If you want to land a 5ft fish you'd better have a big net, and specially designed tackle helps to prevent lost fish.

The Kevlar Grip gloves are ideal for hand-landing catfish.

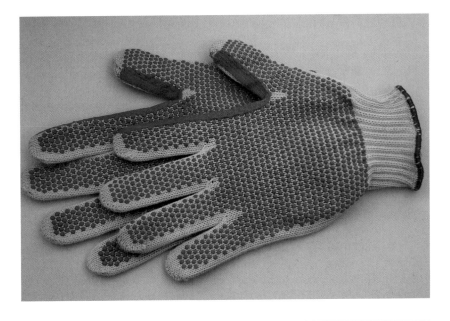

What a beauty! A fish like this deserves careful treatment.

be landed. If it reacts sharply and turns away, it is too fresh to be landed (if a large catfish twists violently it could easily break a wrist). When it is ready to land it will stay still when tapped.

Wait until the fish is quiet and then, with your gloved hand, grab it firmly by the lower jaw. Pull the fish in, using two hands for large fish. Pull it on to an unhooking mat; if it is too heavy to lift, have the unhooking mat partly in the water.

On the Bank

If you fish for catfish – or are fortunate enough to catch one when you are fishing for something else – then you need to consider the care of your catch. Appropriate care is essential to ensure that your catch is returned to the water safely and in good health. The principles here are no different from those associated with any other capture. However, catfish can be large, and they also have particular features (such as abrasive teeth) that warrant extra consideration.

There are a number of key points to consider. Once the fish is in the landing net, lift the fish out carefully and place it on a prepositioned, dampened unhooking mat. Always try to choose a shady spot to unhook your fish in, and keep a bucket of water handy to keep the fish wet.

Many people look at catfish and find their size and large mouth very fearsome, but catfish are one of the most docile fish you will ever see on the bank. Catfish do not bite when out of water, so do not be afraid of them. Their teeth are abrasive pads that will not cause cuts, but they are angled inwards to the mouth so if you do hold a fish in the mouth keep hold and do not pull your hand out sharply as this may cause a minor graze.

Deal with a catfish confidently and it will normally lie quietly on the mat. When it does move it tends to be in one of two ways: it will either 'snake' in a swimming motion, or whip its tail round and go into a horseshoe shape. Catfish do not thrash like carp and so the unhooking mat you use really needs to be long, with a large surface area; these factors are more important than a lot of padding. It appals me to see the number of catfish shown in the angling press which are trailing off a mat on to the ground. Decent catfish unhooking mats are available and are a small price to pay to ensure the safe handling of the fish. If you are caught

without a suitable mat, try laying two together or, in an emergency, you could even use a sleeping bag with a cover over it.

The hook is usually in the side of the mouth and can normally be removed with a pair of strong forceps or long-handled pliers (such as those used for pike fishing). If you are nervous about unhooking catfish, use catfishing gloves (otherwise, simple gardening gloves will suffice). If the hook is deep, remove it with care; in larger fish it may be possible to put your hand down the throat to feel for a deep-set hook, but I would be very careful about doing this.

If you are taking photographs, ensure that you hold the fish over the mat and as low to the ground as possible so that, if it slips, you can

Catfish deserve to be looked after. A proper catfish unhooking mat is a must for all catfish anglers.

The right equipment: the new Catfish-Pro weigh sling amply handles this mid-20lb example.

quickly lower it back on to the mat and then get a better grip.

Keep the fish out of the water for the minimum length of time, and when you put it back ensure that it has fully recovered – if necessary supporting the fish in the water until it is breathing strongly and swims away. When you are supporting a catfish in the water, take care as, occasionally, it will turn and attempt to bite you; it is odd that this happens only when the fish is in the water, never on the bank.

If you have handled catfish before and understand what is required, watch out for any other anglers who may hook and land one: you can then show them how to handle the fish to ensure that it is not mistreated.

Weighing Catfish

Catfish should ideally be weighed in a weigh sling. (The weigh sling is also the safest way to move a catfish around and to take it to the margins for release.) The sling should be up to the job – one that is too small will see the fish sliding out on one side.

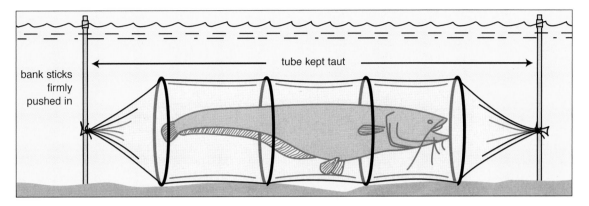

The correct set-up of a catfish tube is essential to ensure fish safety. The tube should be positioned as deeply as possible and monitored carefully for the duration of the fish's retention.

Catfish are slippery and should be handled carefully when unhooking and weighing them. I normally put my weigh sling over the unhooking mat so that it is already in place when I have unhooked the catfish. I can then remove the landing net and just lift the fish up.

Always weigh the fish as quickly as you can, but remember to deduct the weight of the sling after you have weighed the fish in it. If you are caught without a suitable weigh sling, use your landing net to weigh the fish in. If the fish is really big and you have no method of weighing it then you can get a good idea of the weight by measuring its length (*see* box, right).

Watch Out for Stress

Catfish, like many other fish, can become stressed on the bank, so keep fish out of water for as short a time as possible and watch carefully for any colour changes: the flanks starting to lighten or redden is a sure sign of stress, and the fish must be returned immediately.

Retaining Catfish

If you need to retain catfish this should be for only the minimum period required and should be done using appropriate methods.

Suitable Methods

Catfish can be safely retained in two ways:

1. By using a catfish tube.
2. By using a catfish stringer.

Catfish Tube

A catfish tube is like a keepnet except that it is open at both ends. It should be made of a soft, mesh material with plenty of holes to allow for good water exchange.

To prepare the tube for use, first wet it thoroughly and then close one end securely. Place the catfish head first into the other end. Then

---

Estimating Weight

If you have no means of weighing your fish, you can calculate its probable weight from its length. Measure the fish from the tip of the nose to the end of the tail; if you have no tape measure mark it out with bank sticks or your rod.

As a rough guide, the number of centimetres over 1m approximately equates to the weight. For example, 1.3m will be about 30lb, 1.55m will be about 55lb. You can make a judgement to adjust slightly for a particularly thin or fat fish: bulk – or lack of it – is likely to make a 5–8lb difference either way.

The soft nylon stringer is the best and safest way to retain large catfish.

close the open end securely to give you an enclosed tube with the catfish in it.

Next, stake the tube out in the water, using bank sticks at each end. The water should be as deep as possible to ensure a good oxygen level. (*See* diagram on page 89.) Catfish tubes are generally used only in lakes but, if you are fishing a river and wish to retain the fish in a tube, ensure that the tube is set in calm water with the head pointing upstream.

To set the tube up correctly it is recommended that you wade out: you can then check that it is lying reasonably flat and tight, which is important to ensure that the tube retains its shape. Use securely positioned bank sticks at each end of the tube and also an additional safety cord attached to the bank so that if the

bank sticks are knocked out the tube cannot roll down into the lake.

When you come to remove the fish, open the tube at the head end to allow the fish to come straight out.

Catfish Stringer

This is most commonly used for large catfish and in rivers. A stringer should be a thick, soft cord, at least 10m long. One end is passed into the catfish's mouth and out behind the gill cover ahead of the first gill raker. The cord is then tied back to form a loop. The stringer through the mouth should be slightly loose with about 3in play in it. The fish can then be returned to the water and line paid out. Normally, the fish will take the stringer out and then settle quietly; however, in some circumstances the fish may not find a suitable spot and will thrash or continually pull on the stringer. If the fish does not settle quickly reposition it; if it appears stressed, release it.

Once the fish is settled, ensure the stringer is securely tied off at the bank end – to a tree or to an extremely secure bank stick – especially if you have a large fish. When using a stringer ensure that there are no major snags present that could catch the stringer and cause problems when retrieving the fish.

Stringers are most commonly used abroad, but they are also perfectly suitable for use in Britain. Anglers who have not had experience of using them are sometimes reluctant to do so, but when used correctly there should be no issues.

Unsuitable Methods

Catfish should never be held in keepnets. Keepnets are not suitable because it is impossible to set them up in an appropriate way and they are likely to cause stress. Carp sacks should also never be used. If kept in such sacks the fish's abrasive teeth can catch in the limp sacking, which prevents the catfish from being able to breathe properly and so it drowns. Even if the teeth do not catch the sacking, the oxygen exchange can be too poor to enable catfish to breathe adequately. Sacks have unfortunately caused a number of catfish deaths.

With a big fish, getting in the water to have a photograph taken is sensible. If you lose your grip and drop the fish, it will not injure itself in the way it probably would on land.

Photography

Photographing catfish can be tricky: they are big, long and slippery. However, they are generally quiet on the bank and relatively easy to deal with from that point of view.

Most of the weight of a catfish is at its front so, to hold the fish for the photograph, the technique I recommend is to pass one hand under the catfish's head and hold the pectoral fin on the other side of the fish. Its weight is then borne by your wrist and lower arm, making it easier for you to remain balanced. If you find the weight too much you can go on your knees and raise one knee under your hand as extra support.

Your other hand should be placed about two-thirds of the way down the fish so that you can hold the catfish fairly flat with the last third of the tail (the lightest part) able to flop downwards. For the purposes of photography it is important to manoeuvre your hand to ensure that the tail profile is facing the camera.

I almost always have pictures of fish taken when I am on my knees. This way the fish is not too far off the ground, enabling me to lower it if my grip loosens or the fish wriggles. If you

When you come to return your catfish, make sure that it goes back healthy. Support the fish and allow it to recover before releasing it.

A returned catfish rests and gets its bearings in the margins before swimming off.

cannot safely hold the fish, lay it out on the ground before you. With large fish, it is often easier to wade into the water and have the picture taken with the fish there; the potential disadvantage of this is that if you lose your grip on the fish it is likely to escape and swim off.

Returning Catfish

As with all rod-caught fish, catfish will be tired after a fight and may need time to recover before swimming off. For large fish in particular, it is safest and easiest to move the fish around in the weigh sling. You can carry the sling into the water, allow it to fill with water, and then ease the catfish out. Sometimes the fish will immediately shoot off, showering you with water, but most often it will lie quietly. Hold the fish steady and watch to ensure that the gills are moving; allow it time and you will feel it flex before swimming off. Occasionally a fish will roll over a little; if it does, support it upright.

Take particular care when handling a fish in the water as it is the only time that it is likely to have a go. Having said this, while it may try to turn and bite you, it is usually a half-hearted attempt and is nothing to fear.

6 MAGIC SESSION

The biggest impact on the availability of catfish fishing in Britain in recent years has been the development of what are referred to as 'commercial coarse fisheries'. These are typically multi-lake, relatively new fisheries custom-built with excellent on-site facilities (shops, food, WC, and so on); they usually have high fish stock levels and are well promoted. These operations are often forward thinking and seem to have more vision than many of the traditional match-based angling clubs. Many stock catfish in one or more of their lakes and have provided good fishing, albeit at top prices for it.

Elphicks: the First Day

I have always tried to vary my fishing for all species, and I still enjoy some free fishing on small rivers, in club waters and some trips to the commercial coarse fisheries. One such fishery is Elphicks, near Tonbridge in Kent, which contacted me, when they opened, about getting publicity through the Catfish Conservation Group. We helped with this, and the following two years we had CCG fish-ins there. Unfortunately, both occasions proved frustrating with no fish being caught. This is regrettably typical of catfishing at this and other venues – when catfish aren't feeding, you can't catch them, and they do lie up for periods. It also follows that, when catfish come on the feed, if you are in the right place at the right time you can get a good catch. Happily, this is what happened to me a couple of years ago.

After the second blank fish-in, I felt more determined to catch catfish from the lake, especially after seeing the pictures displayed in the fishery shop showing some really nice fish to almost 50lb. I booked up a 36-hour session for myself and Keith in September, and we duly arrived for the session in mild, overcast conditions, with a steady breeze. I had checked the forecast and, while there was rain over 80 per cent of the country, the southeast had been forecast to miss most of it, and so it proved. We arrived late in the afternoon and set up the gear.

As I have said earlier, I believe that watercraft plays a big part in fishing and is often not given the significance it deserves. Before deciding on where and how to fish, it is important to assess the weather conditions, the fishery, the lake, and the techniques and catch rates of other anglers, and to supplement these assessments with your own angling experience and anything you know about other, similar fisheries. On this occasion I had heard that catfish were quite often hooked by carp anglers when fishing method feeders, so I decided to try a new approach. I deduced that the noise of bait going in, the activity of other fish feeding, and the smell release, must have been attracting inquisitive catfish. With this in mind, I took a gallon of maggots and a mixture of feed pellets (trout, carp and halibut in mixed sizes). My aim was to establish a bed of bait to fish on and near. I used a variety of pellets to get a progressive breakdown of bait and ensure a continuing smell release. The pellets with higher oil content would break down more slowly.

Within 30 seconds I discovered that there was a major flaw in this plan – ducks and geese. Within five pouchfuls' going in I had waterbirds streaming from around the lake to feast. A change in tactics was called for and I resorted to sneaking out every ten minutes to put two pouches in, stopping before the birds arrived;

This superb 34-08 catfish was part of my magical session at Elphicks.

this way they would lose interest quickly. I was also able to top the bait up after dark when most of the birds were roosting. I positioned lobworms over the baited area, and livebaits next to it and in open water, and settled in for the first night. Conditions remained mild and I was expecting action soon after dark; but the alarms stayed silent.

I was dozing peacefully when, at 2.30 a.m., I was woken by the scream of the delkim. It was the worm rod. Strike! The rod hooped over and I'm into a good fish, obviously a cat from the hard, bottom-hugging runs. Keith was soon round and I gradually eased the fish into the margins. It was obviously a good fish. 'Looks like a forty,' said Keith, as I netted it. After removing the landing net arms I was able to grip the mesh firmly above the fish and lift it on to the unhooking mat. It felt solid and I thought Keith's estimate was about right. The lovely, pale-mint coloured fish was soon hoisted up to be weighed in at slightly lighter than expected at 37-10. I was chuffed, as it was a British personal best for me. Shortly afterwards, Keith had a take and landed a 23lb fish, but then nothing more for either of us in the night.

The Second Day

Dawn broke with conditions still overcast and grey, but dry. I rebaited the worm rod and topped up the baited area with another two pints of maggots and half a kilo of mixed pellets. As it became fully light I started getting many single beeps and tugs on the worm rod. I reeled in and checked the hook to find that most of the worms had been pecked at or pulled off. I persisted for another three hours with the worm rod, but by mid-morning I had to surrender: the small carp and perch were too active and shredding the worms within 20 minutes of casting. I switched to a small polyballed livebait.

I had a sort-out and sat back to reflect and reconsider the plan for the day. After that I checked and repositioned all the baits, topped up with another few pouchfuls of pellets, and

waited. With overcast conditions and a good chop on the water, I hoped for – rather than expected – a take, so I took the opportunity to reorganize my jumbled tackle bag. But then, at 11 a.m., bang! The left-hand rod with the polyballed livebait over the baited area was away. The firm strike brought an immediate angry slap of a decent catfish's tail (the bait was in only 4ft of water). Again a great scrap and a 34-08 cat graced my net. What a bonus – a cat in the day! Forty minutes later, having taken some photographs and changed out of a slimy T-shirt, I was having a cuppa when, blow me, the same rod was off again (again over the baited area) and I landed another 30-plus catfish (35-08). Three thirties in ten hours! It looked like the cats were on the feed. And certainly I had noticed oil spots regularly coming up over the baited area, indicating fish feeding.

I was sorting out again when Keith gave a shout to say that bacon butties were ready. I walked along to Keith's swim to collect one and had barely got there when my buzzer went off again. 'I don't bloody believe it!' was Keith's understandable response. A short sprint back to my swim next door and I was in time to bend into a scrappy cat, much smaller at 10-08 – this time on a sub-surface bait fished on a dumbell rig straight out away from the baited area. That would surely be it, I thought, and I settled under my brolly as a drizzle set in for the next couple of hours and the ripple on the water increased as the wind freshened. Blow me, when a little later the delkim alarm sounded and the dumbell rig was away again. I hooked into a fish that didn't really do anything: 'It's not that big,' I called to Keith. But after a minute or two it showed me to be no judge of size as it suddenly woke up and went on a 40yd run to my right, flattening the rod.

I had to really clamp down to turn the fish, since it was getting close to a carp angler in the next swim and I didn't want him to get a line bite, strike or possibly cut my line. Thankfully, the fish turned and I worked it back grudgingly towards me. After a last few, short runs I managed to net it. It looked like a biggy and I lifted it out of the water, holding the landing net mesh above the fish. It's a magic moment when you try to lift a fish and find it heavier than you thought; and this was one of those moments. I failed to lift it and had to grip the mesh tighter before I could haul it in. 'Er, it's a big-un,' I said apologetically to Keith, as I carried the lump of a fish out.

It wasn't that long but it was really solid, and we both estimated it at 40–45lb. Wrong. The needle on the reliable Reuben Heaton scales swung further and further round until it stopped at 52-08. I'd got another PB and the fish was a new lake record. I put the fish back in the net to rest while I phoned the fishery owner, Tom, who chugged up in his six-wheel 'Gator' to take some pictures and join in the good-natured banter.

Once the honours were done I took the fish into the water to make sure that it was OK to return. I was just releasing it when another rod went off. I received a lot of genially abusive taunts as I hooked into another cat, which, when landed, turned out to be an 18-pounder. I was wet, covered in slime, and completely happy.

Every time I watch the sun come up at dawn I wonder why I don't get up at that time every day – it's just so beautiful.

My third thirty in ten hours – fantastic.

I had another sort out, washed and changed clothes, and then sat down to work out the details of what had happened that day. Checking my watch it was 5.15 p.m. I calculated that the combined weight of the six catfish I had caught from 15 hours of fishing was 194lb; of this total, 156lb had come in the last six hours. (My two previous visits had totalled 72 hours for no fish.) The sixth fish completed the action for the day, and we fished for the second night, which was unsurprisingly quiet in my swim. Keith hooked but unfortunately lost a cat.

My English PB is this super 52-08 fish from Elphicks, the dumbell rig did the trick again!

Lessons Learnt

Reflecting on the trip, I came to three conclusions. Firstly, the catfish were out on the feed and, on a fishery like this, it is worth fishing it when a couple of fish have been caught recently. Secondly, the overcast, breezy conditions meant the catfish were comfortable coming into shallower water (under 5ft) and taking mid-water and sub-surface baits. Thirdly, the baiting technique I had used seemed to have had a positive

effect – at least it definitely did not have a negative effect – although many further sessions would be needed to validate the method.

I have used the same baiting technique on other sessions on other fisheries since, and I have been successful. However, to prove that there are few sure things in fishing, I returned to the lake at Elphick's in October, in similar conditions, with three other CCG members. We fished for 36 hours for no runs. The conclusion? That's catfishing.

7 CATFISHING IN EUROPE

Outside Britain there is a huge fishing world where wels catfish reach incredible sizes and there are many other big and hard-fighting catfish waiting for you. With angling being so popular in Britain, and comparatively high pressure on our fisheries, the attractions of travelling to the Continent to fish are obvious – the quieter waters, the bigger fish, and the warmer climate. Twenty years ago, few ventured abroad, but today there are thousands of anglers travelling every year to France, Spain and beyond.

For catfish anglers, the scarcity of catfish waters in Britain and the modest size of fish in most of them cause many anglers to look abroad. Catfish angling across Europe is more accessible than it has ever been, making trips there easier than ever before, with better catfishing than ever before. Wels catfishing in Europe involves two types of venue: lakes and rivers. This chapter therefore looks at these – and the techniques and tackle used for them – rather than dealing with individual countries. The methods can then be used wherever you are, with the strength of the tackle used matched to the conditions and the size of fish in the venue you visit.

I have fished abroad for catfish for over 20 years and, though much of it has been hard work, I have enjoyed it immensely. Many people ask if it 'spoils' catfishing for me here; my answer is always that it does not, but each individual will decide this for himself. I do know some anglers who, having travelled to Spain and caught 100lb-plus catfish, now rarely fish for cats in Britain, but they are the minority. Almost all the catfish anglers I know fish both here and abroad.

Beyond Europe there are other catfish species to try for. Some can be found at established fishing destinations with guiding services; others, in

A catfish that changed our horizons: Kevin Maddocks with the first biggy from France, a 70lb catfish from the River Seille, caught over 20 years ago.

My first big catfish was this 84-08 beauty from the river Saône, caught on an October trip.

more remote, less pressured locations, require the angler to rough it in order to gain access. What is for sure is that, if you travel abroad, you have every chance of a great and memorable experience, and usually in beautiful surroundings.

Finding Your Catfish

Across Europe you have a huge choice of fishing. For the biggest catfish, the major rivers are the prime destinations since many of them contain large populations of catfish, including many 100lb-plus fish; however, unless you have a guide you are likely to need a lot of specialist equipment and a boat. Lakes offer some good fishing, where uprated British tackle and tactics will normally do the job, and so these are within

the reach of most anglers and are especially suitable for a first trip.

Rivers

Catfish are an eastern European species, whose natural range extends only as far west as Germany and as far south as Iran and Iraq. Catfish inhabit many of the major rivers of Europe; some of these have native populations and others have had catfish introduced to them.

The primary and most accessible destinations for British anglers are the rivers into which catfish have been introduced: the Ebro in Spain; the Saône/Rhône, Garonne, Loire, Seine and others in France; and the Po in Italy. It is surprising to think that catfish have been in these rivers for no more than 35 years. And yet, in that relatively short time, the Ebro and its tributaries have become the most popular catfishing destination in Europe; it is the river offering the best chance of catching a catfish of over 100lb – the target of a lifetime for most anglers. Unlike the UK's waters, where catfish growth rates have been slow and no river populations have been established, the French, Italian and Spanish rivers in particular have established good populations and offer some great fishing.

As well as these western countries, there is some good catfishing in eastern Europe and beyond, though locating the better venues with big fish requires thorough research and often an investment in pilot trips. The main impact on eastern European fishing has been the amount of commercial fishing. A 100lb catfish is likely to be over 15 years old and therefore will have had to survive a variety of nettings, long lines and other commercial fishing methods. As an example, some years ago I accepted an invitation to evaluate the Danube in Romania as a fishing destination. We were based near Tulcea, following reports of huge catfish there. On our arrival at the river we saw a bustling fish-landing station near by, but, when the time came to fish the river, barely a fish broke the surface. We had hardly a bite by any method, and I came away thinking that I had never fished a river with fewer fish of all species in it. Yet, as we travelled down the river further from the main town, there was obviously a much higher fish population. We fished hard for a week and, between the five of us, caught lots of catfish bigger than about 8lb. I believe that in that river there are a lot of small catfish and a few very large ones that are able to break long lines.

The mighty Danube delta. This is the St Georges arm of the river, which we fished with little success: the area that we were able to fish had been very heavily commercially fished.

Without that trip we would not have been able to discover that situation and realize that a campaign for a big fish would most likely require a long trip down the delta away from the main fishing areas.

The Primary European River Destinations

Spain

The most popular (and heavily fished) river in Europe for catfish is the Ebro and some of its tributaries. It is some 910km (565 miles) long and, with the catfish originally stocked at Mequinenza, the primary population is from

there downstream to the delta, the whole 200km (124 miles) stretch offering great fishing. Catfish have spread upstream to beyond Sastago; the tributaries of the Segre and the Cinca, which join the main river at Mequinenza, also contain large populations and are heavily fished.

The river Ebro has three major dams from Mequinenza downstream to Flix, with weirs above and below the main dammed sections. The flow on the river in the dammed sections is usually slow, particularly since the river system is suffering from much water abstraction to supply the massive fruit orchards that surround the river. There are a large number of guiding companies operating on the river, primarily around Mequinenza and in the delta area around

At the junction of the Segre and the Ebro, the coloured water of the Segre does not immediately mix with the Ebro. The catfish much prefer the warmer, coloured water of the Segre, and the last three miles of the Segre at Mequinenza contain probably the highest density of 100lb-plus catfish in Europe – and the highest density of anglers, too.

The famous catfish hotspot: the foul-smelling chicken-factory outflow on the Ebro at Amposta – Phew!

Tortosa/Amposta. There still remains plenty of river between these areas, with a lot less angling pressure: places such as Asco, Xerta, Mora, Benifalett, Miravet all offer good fishing. The river contains catfish to over 200lb, but the main attraction is that it contains a good population of 100lb-plus fish.

France

Many river systems in France have excellent catfishing potential; they are subject to much less pressure than the Ebro and offer good opportunities for the more adventurous.

The Rhône/Saône system offers the best catfishing, with fish from Dijon on the Saône, all the way down to the confluence with the Rhône at Lyon and the Rhône down into the delta in the Carmargue. The catfish populations are less dense than they are in the Ebro, but this river

system can offer some good fishing (with catfish to over 180lb being caught). The Saône in the Chalon to Mâcon area is the most popular with British anglers – and is a potential area in which to start – but fishing is viable on the whole river. It is a six- to seven-hour drive from Calais to this area, so it is reasonably accessible, and bank access is good. There are currently no British catfishing guides operating on the river.

The Loire has contained catfish for many years, although it is a more difficult river to fish than the Saône as it is mainly shallow and fast flowing. Fish location is critical: fish are mainly to be found in deeper holes and around the confluences with tributaries.

The Lot/Garonne/Dordogne river system has really improved as a catfish venue (with catfish to over 170lb being caught). For most of the lower system, mobile, boat-based fishing is the

The river Saône, probably my favourite. Sometimes kind but often cruel it is home to some lovely catfish.

best approach. It is a fair way south, so accessing it is likely to require your linking up with someone local who can guide you, or embarking on a longer exploratory trip.

The Seine around and above Paris has also come on in recent years and now contains cat-fish to over 100lb; it is very accessible to British anglers and is worthy of investigation.

The Tarn runs through the town of Albi in south-west France. It has had some attention but has hardly been fished by British anglers in recent years; catfish to over 100lb are found there.

Beware the wash from the big barges on the Saône, which can swamp your tackle and wash away keepnets if you are not careful.

Three catfish in four hours from the idyllic Kingfisher lake when filming Passport to Catfish: French Lakes – *a great end to the filming.*

Keith returns a nice Saône fish. On this trip we caught nothing for four days, but by moving regularly we dropped on to some fish on our third spot.

My good friend Alan Kettle-White with a fish from the River Seille, the Saône tributary that we started on before moving to fish the Saône itself.

Bob Baldock with the first big fish we had from the Saône on our first trip, a 72lb beauty.

Richard Garner with a mint 45lb fish.

Pete Shefford with a solid fish. In the early days there were no unhooking mats so a sleeping bag did the trick in an emergency.

Italy

The mighty river Po in northern Italy is one of the most exciting rivers: a big river, it probably contains more 200lb-plus fish than any other. It offers a real angling challenge and for most of its lower stretch requires a boat to be fished effectively. There are a number of fishing camps on the river (but no British-run ones). For the bolder, more experienced catfish angler it has to be on the target list.

Germany/Austria/Hungary/Romania

Many rivers across these countries contain catfish. The most famous (which passes through them all) is the Danube – the river that gave its name to the catfish the Danubian wels.

The Commonwealth of Independent States and Beyond

All the major rivers in the CIS, the successor body to the USSR, contain catfish and offer a challenge for the more adventurous. The main destination for catfish anglers has been the river Volga delta, around Astrakhan, where a number of camps have operated. The whole delta has a

Kevin Maddocks with the biggest fish of the trip to the Volga Delta: an old-looking one of 132lb.

The River Po in Italy had produced a huge number of big fish. A river I plan to revisit, it has the best potential for world-record fish.

massive catfish population, including some really big fish, though it is heavily fished commercially.

In Kazakhstan the river Lli has attracted a number of intrepid anglers to brave the long journey; many big fish have been caught, to over 200lb. There are some camps on the river because guiding is essential.

Most of the other rivers across the CIS and other eastern European countries contain catfish, but it takes patience and investigation to track down viable angling destinations.

Lakes

Lakes and reservoirs certainly offer anglers a lot more than rivers in that the waters are enclosed, though they often take as much investigation and probing to verify the stocking density of catfish and their size. (One famous continental fishery advertised for several years by showing an image of a huge catfish being stocked into the lake, when, in fact, the fish had died three days later and no other fish were anywhere near as big.)

The huge number of lakes in Continental Europe means that it is not feasible to list them here, but France is far and away the most popular venue for British anglers travelling to lakefish, and there are a wide variety of well-run fisheries across the country to choose from.

Many other countries also have viable fisheries with catfish in them, particularly the old Eastern Bloc countries – such as the Czech Republic, Romania, Hungary, Slovenia, and Slovakia. As with rivers, any potential fishery should be investigated as much as possible before you travel to it to validate stock levels and recent captures. Many have undertaken long trips only to find that the stock levels are much lower than expected.

The delta boats were our fishing base for ten days on the Volga – numb bums all round.

Double delight: two nice fish to start the Passport to Catfish: French Lakes *filming from* Le Bounty.

The first catfish over 200lb known to have been caught by an English angler was this 202lb monster, caught by Kevin Maddocks in Kazakhstan, which at the time was an IGFA record.

For British anglers, the main advantage of visiting Continental lakes (rather than rivers) is that they can be fished using techniques, tackle and approaches very similar to those used in Britain: the predominance of lake carp and catfish in Britain gives British anglers a sound basis for fishing lakes abroad, although bigger fish are likely to need heavier gear.

Choosing Your Destination

The most accessible fishing requiring the least change of tactics is offered by France. Most of these are carp and catfish lakes, offering great mixed fishing and allowing you to fish for both species or just for catfish. Many people have a week in France as a fishing holiday and you can choose from a wide variety of venues, from those within one or two hours of Calais, to those that are an eight- or nine-hour drive away. Spending a week at one site can be really enjoyable, allowing time to bait up areas and vary your tactics, and giving you a great chance of catching. You can find a huge number of managed lake destinations in France and beyond on the internet, through the angling press and at angling shows.

Before deciding on a venue, find out as much as possible about it, and take into account factors such as cost, distance, time available, the availability of guiding services (if required), angling pressure, and quantity and size of fish.

Budget
Your budget may dictate the venue and the style of fishing you choose. Travelling to Spain for a

fully guided week's fishing is likely to cost significantly more than it would for six people to book a lake in France and share travel.

Time

The amount of time you have is an important consideration when planning trips. If you have plenty of time you are more able to try new venues, explore and experiment, which may result in finding some great fishing with little pressure on the venue. If you are short of time and want to maximize your fishing time you may want to choose a place that is easily accessible and can provide gear, allowing you to travel

quickly and begin fishing immediately. For this kind of trip, the Ebro is an ideal potential venue: you can get an early flight from Britain and be out fishing by early afternoon, with the same fast return time, making a three- or four-day trip possible.

Angling Pressure

I know many anglers whose primary reason for fishing abroad is to get away from the crowded fisheries at home to quieter ones abroad. The ability to rent a whole lake of, say 8 acres with just five anglers, or to fish a river where you cannot see another angler is greatly preferable to

There is some fantastic catfishing to be had in many lakes across France. Most waters have suffered considerably less pressure and contain larger fish than those in Britain. They are well worth considering for a holiday trip.

122lb of fast-water catfish from the 'Passport to Catfish Spain: The Ebro'. This fish was hooked in 4ft of water and had to be played across a current you'd normally expect to be barbel-fishing in.

some. There are many places abroad for this and, even on the heavily fished Ebro, there are areas of little pressure in the middle-lower reaches.

Size and Quantity of Fish

If you want to target catfish specifically it is well worth trying to find out as much as you can about the stock before you travel, particularly if you plan to fish a lake where catfish have been stocked. A fishery's advertising tag line, 'Carp to 50lb and catfish to 100lb,' gives no information on stocking levels of either species. In some fisheries, as in Britain, a relatively low number of catfish are stocked to offer a novelty species for carp anglers, but the numbers may not be sufficient to make a viable target for a catfish expedition. It is reasonable to say that most of the

really big catfish (125lb-plus) are to be found in rivers, and so that is a better target. However, to locate fish on rivers is much harder on all but the most heavily fished areas and so may require a lot of research and fishing to find the producing areas. The Saône has proved to be a river that produces more fish to regular anglers who have located fish-holding areas and use appropriate techniques; the rewards are rich if you can get it right.

If catfish are not your main target species but may be present when you are carp fishing, then to put one rod out for catfish can be an excellent starting point.

Once you have an idea of the type of trip you would like, look in more detail at the destinations on offer.

Worth a kiss! I hooked this 69lb fish on a light drachkovich set-up when zander fishing and landed it 40 minutes later, three miles downstream.

In Spain some fish are very yellow, such as this small one.

A rare moment: a 'double hook up'. John Wilson and Gary Allen both into fish on the upper Ebro.

The Bavarian Guiding Service base, the first and still the largest fishing camp at Mequinenza has provided me with some memorable trips.

Style of Fishing – Guided or Not?

There are two types of trip to big rivers: guided and unguided. Guiding can be essential at venues where boats and specialist gear are required. If you are new to catfishing, or do not have a lot of time to travel to Europe, then guiding services can be invaluable as tackle and airport pick-ups are often provided, making even a three- or four-day trip a realistic possibility.

The primary advantage of guided fishing is that it avoids the problems associated with not knowing your venue: this is in the hands of someone local, able to adjust tactics to conditions. For example, if you arrive and a river is running high, a local guide is likely to have encountered the conditions before and be able to advise and assist in location and methods to catch fish, maximizing your fishing effectiveness.

Guides can normally supply or help with the sourcing of bait; and they will usually also provide or rent suitable tackle, so that if you are fishing alone the cost of specialist tackle is minimized. However, if you are fishing frequently you may find that you prefer to have your own gear. Guides can also normally obtain the necessary fishing permits for you in advance, saving hassle and delays.

Guiding services are broadly advertised and promoted in the angling press, and most have a website. I would always advise that you should speak to the operators to understand the style of fishing, facilities and packages on offer before choosing. Several of the main operators have

The biggest catfish I have seen – 187lb, from the Segre, caught on rubber shad.

Gently does it Simon! This 118lb fish was caught just six weeks after I had been in hospital for a week for the removal of my burst appendix. Gary had struck the rod for me and I had played it very carefully. Having booked the trip, I didn't want to miss it.

Fancy fishing in your wedding gear! Catfish fanatics Kevin and Tracey Midmore with an awesome 'albino' catfish from Spain – what a honeymoon!

stands at the major angling shows (during the winter and early spring) so you also have the opportunity to visit and speak to them in person. Some tackle shops also have links with holiday companies.

Remember that as well as fully guided packages, some guiding companies will also offer separate boat/tackle/accommodation rental and help with licences, providing a handy base for those who want to fish on their own but need local services at their destination.

The Ebro and some other European rivers (the Po and the Lli) have many fishing camps offering guided fishing. These venues are typically a flight or two away from Britain. For most European rivers, however, there are virtually no fishing camps or guides and you face a solo trip if you want to try them. This should not in itself

dissuade you, but such ventures do require a considered approach and planning, and they often necessitate repeat trips to find the best areas and get to grips with a river's moods and the catfish habits. However, the rewards can be rich and, for some anglers, the point of travelling abroad is to fish away from other people and go their own way. They feel that the fish caught are worth more if they have done all the work, so they derive a greater sense of achievement from any captures made on solo trips.

My view is that there are benefits to both. Guided trips are quite social and a good way to get used to a style of fishing, enabling you to go back under your own steam if you prefer. Indeed, many of the guiding companies will rent gear and or boats if you prefer to fish yourself but still want to fly in with a minimum of gear.

I love catfishing.

Going Solo

For the more adventurous who are planning to go it alone, a considerable amount of research is required. First you have to choose your river or lake – which you will know something about – then comes the investigation and planning stage. Identify an area or areas you want to target by checking up on any previous trips, articles, word of mouth, web forums, email and through the tackle trade. The CCG can be a real help here: they are likely to have links with anglers who have fished many of the unguided destinations.

The main destinations are the river systems. Find out as much as you can about river levels at various times of the year as big rivers can flood easily and render fishing difficult. If a river is liable to flooding it may make sense to plan a fall-back venue (another river or lake) in case of problems. If you are travelling a fair way, make your stay as long as possible to enable you

to get the feel of a new venue and to maximize your chances of catching.

To identify licence requirements and local fishing rules may prove difficult, but a visit to a local tackle shop in the nearest town will usually provide information and licences or directions on where to buy licences.

Tips for the Travelling Angler

When travelling abroad you need to plan carefully because items you need cannot always be found at the venue, particularly if you are in one of the less popular localities. In addition to your fishing tackle, there are a number of essential and/or useful items:

- Passport (check the expiry date well in advance of your planned trip).
- Travel insurance.

Trevor Pritchard with a huge Saône moggie of 130lb, what a fish!

- First-aid kit and painkillers.
- Heavy-duty cutting pliers (capable of cutting a big hook in case you catch yourself by accident).
- Weather protection kit (for hot sun and torrential rain).
- Information on where to obtain your licences.
- Information on the local fishing regulations.
- Mobile phone: make sure it is set up for calling from abroad.
- Insect repellent.
- Bait and bait-snatching fishing tackle.
- Film and batteries.
- Life jackets, if boat fishing.

If Driving
- Driving licence and insurance documents.
- Items required by law if driving abroad (for instance, warning triangle, spare bulbs, headlamp beam adjusters and reflective jackets); bear in mind that requirements may vary from country to country.
- Car recovery and trailer (for instance, an AA 5-Star policy).
- Maps (large scale can be useful for exploring rivers).
- GPS is helpful for locating remote fisheries.

If Flying
- Check weights before you travel.
- Check the procedures/charges for outsize luggage.

Kevin Maddocks admires the first big fish caught on our first trip to the Ebro, 69lb.

- Buy or borrow a strong rod case for protecting your rods.

Tackling Up for Big Catfish

The tackle you require will depend on the style of fishing you use and whether you are on a lake or a river. However, the weight of the tackle should be increased as the size of the fish you are likely to catch increases. The various set-ups, summarized in Table 7 (*see* opposite), are described below.

Set-Ups

Set-Up A

If you are fishing a lake with catfish up to 60lb you can use English carp or pike tackle, although I would recommend the use of a stronger mainline than usual, something around 20lb, a tough, robust mono such as Big Game or Pro-Gold, as opposed to a low-diameter line. If you are using braid as a mainline you should approximately double the strength of the mono, so a 40lb braid should be suitable. The hooklink should be heavier to cope with abrasive teeth and, if a braid, a catfish-suitable one.

Set-Up B

With this – a bank fishing set-up with a bank catfish rod or spod rod – you are likely to be in for a long fight if you hook a big fish, but the tackle should be up to it. You may need to be wary of snags and islands as your ability to stop a big fish on a set-up like this is likely to be limited.

Set-Up C

This is a basic set-up balanced to enable you to stand up effectively to a strong catfish, but always bear in mind that a 100lb fish is about 6ft long and very muscular and you need the right tackle. As an example, for the *Passport to Catfish: French Lakes* DVD I fished with set-up B and took 25 minutes to land a 60lb catfish with a lot of hauling and effort. Later that evening I hooked a 69lb catfish on set-up C, landed the

Table 7 Basic Tackle Summary

A	*Tackle:*	standard carp tackle rods 11–12ft, 2.5–3.0lb test curve rod with large carp reel and 20–25lb line
	Fish size:	up to 60lb
	Venues:	lakes and bank fishing on rivers (bank fishing on rivers is always best if you have access to a boat to play the fish from)
	Hooklink:	25lb mono, 50–70lb braid
B	*Tackle:*	rods 11–12ft, 3.5–5lb test curve, big pit-style reel with large capacity 25–30lb line
	Fish size:	up to 90lb
	Hooklink:	30lb mono, 70–120lb catfish braid
C	*Tackle:*	catfish rod 50–200g casting weight, approximately 10ft, multiplier, 80lb braid
	Fish size:	up to 120lb
	Venues:	lakes and bank fishing on rivers (see note above)
	Hooklink:	40lb mono, 120–150lb catfish braid
D	*Tackle:*	catfish rod, 50–300g casting weight, approximately 10ft, multiplier, and 120lb braid
	Fish size:	up to 200lb
	Venues:	bank and boat fishing on rivers (see note above)
	Hooklink:	40lb mono, 150–220lb catfish braid
E	*Tackle:*	catfish/boat rod, 50–300g casting weight, 7–9ft, multiplier, 120–150lb braid
	Fish size:	up to 200lb-plus
	Venues:	boat fishing on rivers
	Hooklink:	40lb mono, 150–220lb mono

fish in under ten minutes and never really lost control of the fish – the rod did a lot more of the work than it did when I used the lighter set-up.

Set-Up D

This slightly heavier set-up for river fishing takes account of the extra strain the current places on tackle, giving you more power and robustness to stop fish in a flow and work them upstream. This set-up can be used for bank fishing; its use for boat fishing is limited. It does offer flexibility when float fishing from a boat (it enables you to hold the bait away from the boat when trotting) and it offers good line pick-up, but it is limited when fighting fish as it is longer than ideal for playing fish from a boat, and care must be taken when fish come close to the boat. This would be an ideal set-up for fishing buoy rigs/tie-up rigs.

Boy, can it rain in France! So go prepared.

Set-Up E

A true boat fishing set-up for legering or float fishing, hefty enough to handle any catfish you are likely to encounter.

Catfish Rods

Specially designed catfish rods are most suitable to combat the power of big catfish. Ideally, such a rod should be in the 4–10oz casting-weight range, considerably heavier than a carp or pike rod and normally shorter at 9–11ft. It should have a grip above the reel set for holding when you are playing the fish; this will impart more pressure and enhance your comfort. It should also be rung so that it can accommodate fixed spool reels or multipliers. The heavier rods should preferably be set up for multipliers.

Reels

The larger the catfish the greater the strain on your tackle; reels especially will take a great deal of punishment. If you are using fixed-spool reels, ensure they are well made as they will have to tolerate a lot of pressure when you are playing fish. Metal spools are a must (plastic ones can be

crushed by the line pressure). For fish up to 70lb you can get by with a carp reel, but for bigger fish I would not recommend anything other than the Shimano bait-runner 4500B or ideally the 6500B, which have both demonstrated the ability to perform under duress. Multipliers, with their line capacity and rugged drag systems (lever or star drag) are most suitable for the heavy end of catfishing. Many of the reputable brands are suitable, but avoid the cheaper ones as these do not stand up well. Multipliers come with or without line guide; if you have not used multipliers much then choose one with a guide as these are simpler to use.

Main Lines

When using heavier lines, braids are usually the most practical option because their narrower diameter allows greater line capacity and reduces the drag when river fishing. Adjust the braid strength to balance your tackle: 40–80lb for heavy bank rods; 80–150lb for heavy bank and boat fishing. For lake fishing, when line capacity is not such an issue, use 20–25lb mono on lighter set-ups and up to 40lb on heavier catfish rods.

Top guide Gary Allen has helped us to catch some excellent fish over many trips to the Ebro.

If you are travelling abroad by vehicle, the larger the better.

Hooks

As with fishing in Britain, the hook size will be determined buy the bait size you are using (typically between a 1/0 and a 10/0, with most fishing done with 4/0 and 6/0 hooks).

Other Terminal Tackle

The remainder of the terminal tackle will need to be uprated from British tackle to suit the larger baits you are likely to use and the bigger fish you expect to encounter. Catfish will test your tackle to the limit so ensure that you have the right gear:

- Very strong swivels and link swivels.
- Big floats to support large livebaits.
- Big in-line leads for legering and for the big floats.
- Heavy-duty rubber beads to act as shock absorbers.
- Bait-shields.
- Catfish hooks that will not straighten.
- Power gum or other braid for stop-knots.
- Rig rattles – a great enhancement to livebait rigs.
- Buoys and 6–8lb break-line if you are buoy-rig fishing.
- Big leads for river legering.

Fish-Handling Equipment

You need to plan how you are going to play, land, handle, retain and weigh your fish, so consider the following:

- Butt pad to save painful bruising.
- Big landing net or glove to hand-land fish.
- Big unhooking mat.
- Big weigh sling.
- Adequate scales, or strong weigh bar or hook.
- Stringer or large catfish tube if retaining fish.
- Photographic equipment.
- Leatherman multi-tool and/or heavy duty pliers for hook removal.

Other Accessories

- GPS: if you are travelling to a large lake or river this may be useful for plotting fishing areas.

Remember that while you can put fresh mono line on to a reel and use it immediately, braided lines are best worked on before use. Load the line wet, then go out and cast and retrieve 20 or 30 times at least to help remove any coating on the braid; it will then lie better on the spool and you are less likely to get the line trapped (which inhibits casting and the playing of fish).

Hooklinks

You can use either mono or catfish hooklinks, depending on the rig and bait. On most occasions catfish-braided hooklinks will be suitable. Only if you are using British-style polyball rigs with smaller baits will mono be more suitable. For float fishing and buoy-rig style fishing, braided hooklinks are fine and offer better bait presentation than monos do.

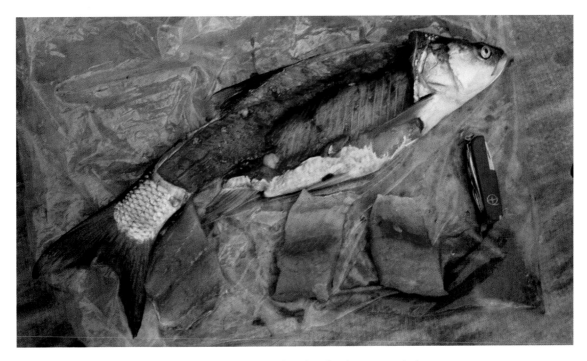

On the Volga we started by catching these large asps and cutting chunks to use as bait.

- Inflatable boat or bait boat.
- Bait-retention equipment – particularly for rivers and when fishing in warm climates, including collapsible buckets, batter air pumps and livebait nets.
- Waterproof bags – for camera equipment, for instance, when you are on a boat.

Baits

Baits have been fully covered in Chapter 3, and there is little to add that is specific to fishing abroad other than that fish baits – live, dead, and cut – are used most widely.

Static Baits

When lake fishing, you can use British methods of baiting up and fishing over a baited area, particularly if the lake is also carp fished and is receiving large amounts of anglers' bait. The advantage of this method if you are on a long session is that the catfish have plenty of time to locate and feed on your baited area. You can keep topping up a baited area, watch out for fish activity, and keep one rod over the bait. If you start getting action then you can switch one or more rods to that area. It is not worth putting all your rods over the baited area as catfish can often take a number of days before they begin to feed well at a baited area; if you have all your rods in the one area you may miss out on chances elsewhere. The actual bait used in the area is not too critical since its purpose is simply to attract fish in.

Static baits may also work on rivers if enough are put in. On the Ebro at Mequinenza a large number of catfish are now caught by using beds of pellets with pellets/squid/deadbait hookbaits over the top. The catfish responded to this method in the months after the marked increase in carp fishing on the river had resulted in boilies, pellets and particles being loose-fed in increasing quantities. However, after only three years of good catch rates on pellet fishing, the catch rates have fallen as the fish have become

The Volga is alive with small catfish; we stopped using cut fish to avoid this type of fish, which plagued us.

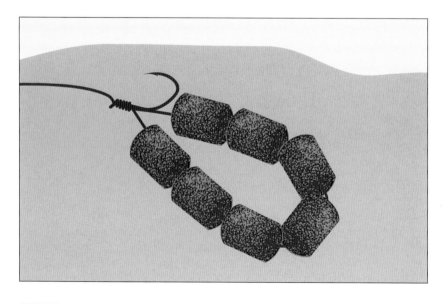

In Spain, some anglers fish a 'necklace' of baits: drilled pellets threaded on to a loop hair. As catfish have become more used to pellet rigs, this has become less effective.

Richard Garner with the catfish he wasn't sure he'd hooked. This fish took at the end of a 150-yard trot, and swam upstream as Richard retrieved the float; it was only when it was 30 yards from the boat that we realized that there was definitely a fish on.

used to the method and are more wary. Pellets have been tried on other rivers to date but with no significant success.

Livebaits

Livebaits have proved to be far and away the most successful catfishing bait used across Europe and are usually the catfish angler's first choice. They can usually be caught or purchased at or near the destination and can be critical for a successful trip, so always plan your bait fishing, get advice and take the best tackle you can.

On my last trip to the Ebro, I found that by using a very soft, quiver-tip rod, small cage feeder and a long tail, I was able to catch at least twice as many small carp for bait than the other bait-fishing anglers were (the others mostly

used method feeders and waited for runs). Most of the bites that I had pulled the quiver tip no more than 2in. Remember – minimum time bait fishing equals maximum time catfishing. Always take back-up bait in case of real problems (frozen deadbaits/squid, lobworms or leeches are ideal). Leeches are suitable for lakes and slow-moving rivers, and, like lobworms, are best kept cool.

Methods

Legering

Legering techniques, which have been covered in Chapter 4, may be used abroad, particularly for lake fishing. Polyball rigs, dumbell rigs and

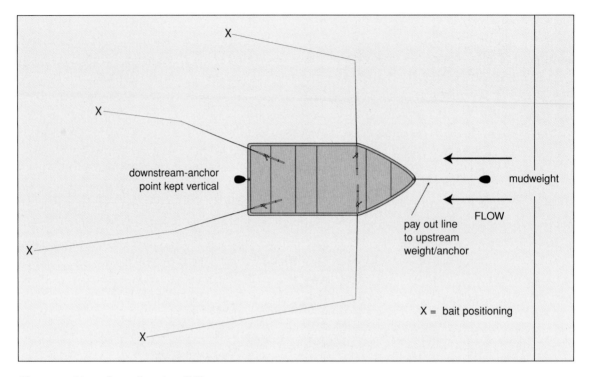

downstream-anchor
point kept vertical

mudweight

pay out line
to upstream
weight/anchor

FLOW

X = bait positioning

How to position a boat when river fishing.

cat-o-copters have all proved effective. You need to be more careful when legering in rivers to take account of the flow on the rig and to cope with friction on the line (causing drag).

If using a polyball rig the in-line variety should be used to minimize tangles. If you are legering eels, running leger rigs with in-line leads are most effective (again to minimize tangling). Sink and draw is also worth trying if you have suitable deadbaits and can cast to 'catfishy spots'.

Float Fishing

For river fishing, this is one of the main methods used abroad, particularly from boats. You can float-fish in a variety of styles to cover the water in different ways. It is a particularly exciting method as you manoeuvre your bait to the position where you think the fish will lie, drifting it round an eddy or trotting along a tree line. Any unusual movement in the float sets your heart racing, and takes look great; it is a much more active style of fishing than sitting behind a bite alarm. Slider floats and big, in-line leads matched to the bait size are the order of the day for float fishing.

Free Roving

If you are fishing an eddy or backwater that has either no flow or a circular flow you can allow the livebait to drift around, adjusting it carefully to get it to cover an area and to go close to fishy spots. You can float-fish from boats while drifting either on the wind across large lakes and reservoirs or down a river current. It is useful when doing this to have an echo sounder to monitor the depth and to watch for snags. This also enables you to reposition and to trot down over a fishy spot, if you so wish, after you have drifted over it.

This method is good for covering large areas of water and, in conjunction with the clonk, it is great fun.

Rather than drifting down a stretch if you want to fish it repeatedly, you can trot baits down when you have sufficient flow. The most common places to do this are where there are overhanging trees that catfish may be sheltering under or where there are deeper areas of a river where catfish are likely to lie up. Alternatively, it could just be an area where you have previously caught fish when drifting and want to cover again.

To trot effectively, position your boat with the bow pointing into the current, and anchor up. For preference fish with two anglers, one fishing from each side of the boat and holding rods parallel to the current to get a reasonable distance between the baits. Slightly longer rods of 10ft are more useful for float fishing from boats than are normal 7–9ft boat rods, as they increase your ability to work bait down the swim (by mending the line or occasionally holding back to let the bait come up in the water). Depending on the flow and the size of the bait, you may need a heavy lead to keep the bait down. On gravel, if there is not too much flow, you can work a bait down the swim by setting your float 2–3ft over depth and laying on. To move the bait, lift up and hold back, allowing the lead to move downstream.

A reel with a decent line capacity is essential for this method because, if you hook a good

fish towards the end of the trot and it goes downstream, it may be a while before you can up-anchor and follow it down.

Clonking

One of the most unusual and exciting methods of catfishing is 'clonking'. On its day, it is easily the most deadly method. It involves the use of a specially carved clonk, or *butschalo*, which is punched into the water to create a popping sound. As the sound is made there are also strong vibrations sent down into the water to which catfish respond. By respond I mean that the fish will lift off the bottom and swim towards the sound, often coming from 30ft down to within a couple of feet of the surface.

Clonking is a well-established technique. How it was originally conceived is unknown, but it was certainly being used at least 50 years ago and probably much before that. The noise of the clonk is similar to the slapping sound of ripples striking a small boat, and I believe that the technique is likely to have been developed to imitate that noise. I say this because many times, when there is the slapping of ripples against a boat, catfish will surface close to the boat and even attack

To use the clonk needs practice. Successful clonking is 'all in the wrist': the clonk is smoothly punched into the water with a stiff wrist, then flicked out by breaking the angle of the wrist. The procedure is carried out in one movement. Good clonking action will result in a popping-type noise; poor clonking just gets you soaked!

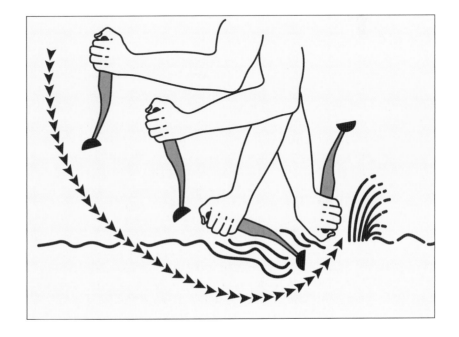

Our first encounter with clonking was during our trip to the Danube delta. Here, Robert Coote thrashes the water to a foam.

it. This is most common in areas where catfish have not been fished for and so the sound is new.

Some believe that the clonk was developed to imitate the sound of a catfish striking at a bait on the surface and thus it is a feeding stimulus; indeed, the sound is similar, though I disagree with this view as catfish soon become accustomed to the clonk noise and cease to respond. If the noise were a true feeding stimulus it would continue to work. In addition, there is the fact that on many occasions when you clonk, many fish respond and yet you do not get a take.

It is a technique whose effectiveness is hard to believe, even when you can see catfish coming to the echo sounder screen – until you get a take. In most rivers, medium and large catfish have no natural predators, and since they are inquisitive they respond to unusual noises. Examining the technique in more detail, clonking is normally a river method, carried out when drifting down a river. It is best used in conjunction with an echo sounder so that you can monitor the river depth, spot large snags (and be ready to lift rigs away from them) and, most importantly, so that you can see when catfish are responding and how far up the fish are swimming. If you know what depth the catfish are at you can position your bait close to that area to maximize your chance of a take. In general, if the river has not been clonked before or only recently you can expect fish to respond aggressively and swim up close to the surface, whereas on regularly fished stretches you will often see the fish move only a few feet off the bottom.

Success! The first fish we caught clonking, but unfortunately rather small. The area we fished had been heavily commercially fished and seemed devoid of bigger fish.

The rod set-ups for clonking usually involve float fishing or suspending a bait with just a large (4–8oz) in-line lead (in essence, float fishing without a lead). The latter method allows you to adjust your depth quickly. Braided line is used to minimize the drag, and a handy hint is to mark the braided line every metre in one colour and every 5m in another so that you can easily calculate the depth to fish at.

A typical scenario would be to drift down a river using one rod per angler, with one man monitoring the echo sounder and regularly calling out the depth and any snags. The anglers then position their baits at a variety of depths. Catfish appear on the screen and the echo-sounder man calls out catfish at, say, 6m; the anglers then adjust their line to around that depth, and wait. One rod is used per angler since takes are sometimes very soft and usually quick, with the fish seldom hanging on. A variety of baits may be used, most typically worms, squid or livebaits.

Clonking can and has been used to good effect on large reservoirs on a drift or slow troll. If used in conjunction with GPS, careful monitoring and recording can identify fish-holding areas, which can then be revisited and fished with other

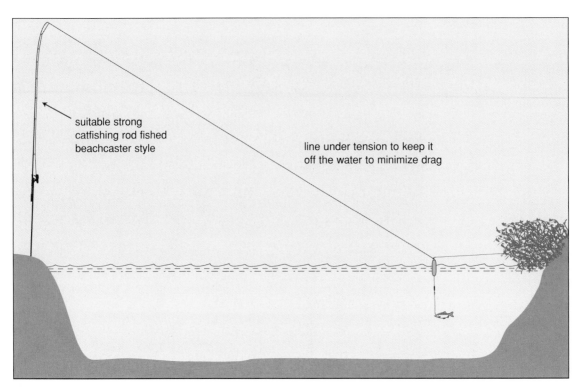

The buoy rig has accounted for countless catfish.

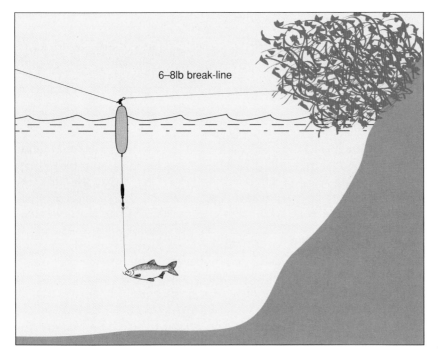

6–8lb break-line

The rig can be tied to trees, or a buoy can be positioned in open water.

Table 8 Using the buoy rig

Problem	Solution	Lake/river
Drag from flowing river	Braided mainline fished under tension keeps it clear of water	River
Debris flowing down river	As above	River
Controlling large livebaits that keep pulling leads	The tethered rig can control the largest baits	Both
Cannot cast out heavy baits	Position baits with a boat	Both
Hook penetration for baits fished at extreme distance (100–150yd)	Mainline fished very tight; when break-line breaks, fish are often automatically hooked	Both
Boat fishing not allowed	Use this method to fish beyond casting range	Both
No boats allowed at all	Method cannot be used; unless a novel method of getting baits out (lilos have been used, though this is dangerous and not recommended)	Both
Fish spook from anglers in boats	Row quietly, put baits out early; once bait positioned, angler returns to the bank, so there is no water disturbance	Both
I want to fish sub-surface 100yd out where I have seen fish striking	The rig enables you to fish the bait at any depth; use a float to suit bait size	Both

methods. Huge areas of water can be covered efficiently by clonking and, on a new stretch, it can be used with reasonable confidence to confirm (or not) the presence of catfish.

Buoy Rigs/Tie-up Rigs

One of the most effective catfishing techniques, originally developed by Dutch anglers on the Ebro, is the buoy rig or tie-up rig. The only difference between the two terms is that, with the former, the break-line is tied to a buoy placed out in the river, and with the latter it is tied off to reeds or trees on a far bank or island. For simplicity I shall refer to the technique from here on as buoy-rig fishing.

Buoy rigs enable you to fish from the bank and yet position a float-fished bait in a fixed place literally anywhere on a lake or river. It is primarily a livebaiting method, but it has occasionally been used for fishing deadbaits on rivers. The technique allows you to overcome a number of difficulties when positioning your bait exactly where you want it.

The set-up is as follows: the rod is placed on a heavy-duty buoy-rod rest able to cope with the tension of the rig. (The buoy-rod rest is angled

133

Buoy-rigged rods need to be held under tension to keep the line off the water and to avoid drag. The boat is ready for playing the fish as this area was snaggy, so we had to take the boat out to land them.

Since the rod is fished under tension, the buoy-rod holder needs to be heavy duty. The plastic tube on the handle prevents the cork from being damaged by the holder. The holder should be angled slightly forward.

slightly forward.) The rod butt is placed in the cup at the bottom and the handle, or blank, rests against the 'V'. If the rod blank rests there, put extra padding on the V of the rest and the rod to avoid damage. The set-up is a standard float fishing one with the addition of a flying swivel loose above the stop-knot for the float.

The break-line of 6–8lb mono can then be tied to the flying swivel. To put the rig out, one angler stands on the bank with the rod while the second one takes the float end of the tackle and rows out to the fishing spot. If the fishing spot is

in open water, a buoy is put in the water, with a rope tied to a mud weight or anchor to hold it in position. The break-line is then tied to the buoy.

The angler on the bank then tightens up the rig. The flying swivel, now under tension, will slide down the line to rest above the stop-knot. Under medium tension the rod is put on the buoy rest and the line is then tightened until it lifts clear of the water. Lastly, a rod bell (for bite indication) is clipped to the top of the rod.

If you are positioning your bait close to trees or reeds instead of on open water, you can simply

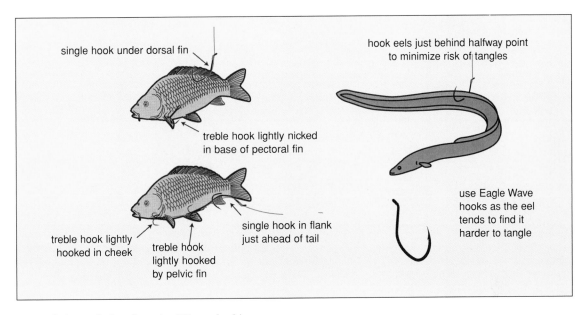

single hook under dorsal fin

treble hook lightly nicked
in base of pectoral fin

treble hook lightly
hooked in cheek

treble hook
lightly hooked
by pelvic fin

single hook in flank
just ahead of tail

hook eels just behind halfway point
to minimize risk of tangles

use Eagle Wave
hooks as the eel
tends to find it
harder to tangle

Larger baits used abroad require different hooking arrangements.

tie your break-line to overhanging branches or reeds. Break-line for buoys or tie-ups should be about 6ft long to allow the rig to pull clear of snags and of the rope holding the buoy.

Hooking Arrangements
Catfish almost always take the bait from underneath, so the hooking arrangements on buoy-rigs are usually multiple hook rigs (depending on the bait size) with at least one hook on the underside of the bait.

Takes from Catfish
By using the buoy-rig fishing method you will experience a variety of types of take; however, usually any take is preceded by the bait's sensing danger and starting to become more active, causing the rod tip to bounce and the bell to jingle a little. This is your wake-up call.

Position yourself by the rod and get ready for one of the following four types of take:

1. Catfish takes bait and swims away from the trees or buoy.
   In this instance the break-line will snap, the rod will spring back, the line will go slack (owing to the lack of tension) and the bell will sound loudly. Action time! Grab the rod and wind vigorously until you are in contact with the fish, and then pump.
2. Catfish takes bait and swims away from you.
   When this happens the rod will just bend and bend, usually going over smoothly and firmly. Before the rod reaches the horizontal, grab it and strike. When you have done this, be careful because in some instances the break-line will not have broken and you may have to pull or strike again to snap it. When this type of take happens you do not have the bell sounding as the rod tends to go over smoothly, so be aware of this and watch the rod tip. Head torches are handy for this at night.
3. Grab and rattle.
   Sometimes a fish will grab a bait and either hold it or shake it, causing the rod bell to sound. This is usually the result of smaller catfish takes, but not always. At this point you have to make a judgement on whether to risk a strike or wait for a full take. It is hard to advise what to do with this sort of take since they can vary so much but, on balance, it is usually better to wait.

On a recent trip we tried trolling lures and, despite poor conditions, had this huge fish, caught by Graham Lawrence. The fat belly indicates a fish that had fed regularly on big beds of pellets; but the capture proved they could be readily caught by other methods still.

Careful Wilson! A catfish close to the boat is the time to be very careful: they are rarely ready to be landed when they first come up. To minimize the risk of lost fish and broken tackle, prepare yourself by loosening your clutch slightly and being ready for a violent lunge.

Top Ebro guide Colin Bunn helps Reg Whitehouse to display this Spanish fish of 224lb.

Linda Billington with the 209lb catfish she caught in 2007 – as far as I know the largest catfish to have been caught by a lady angler.

Guided fishing can get you dream catches. The hardworking John Deakin congratulates a customer on a huge catfish.

Smiles all round!

A personal best, a 155lb catfish when filming Passport to Catfish: Spain: the Ebro, *with help from the Catfish Capers team.*

Many of the xanthochroistic catfish on the Ebro change colour over their lives; this one currently has a lot of natural colour on it.

Huge rainfall and floods in northern Spain resulted in this rare sight – all four sluices of the dam at Mequinenza fully open.

Lure Fishing

Lure fishing is possible at many destinations across Europe, and yet it is the method least used by British anglers. Big rivers and lakes will have large areas with no catfish; thus, fish location is the primary task. Lures are very effective at covering large areas of water, and catfish will take them; they can be bank-fished or trolled. Once fish are located you can always switch to other methods.

Generally, spoons and spinners and shads are used, though trolled plugs and bulldawg-type

Having fished with John Wilson for over 20 years on his local waters, it was fantastic to take John on his first trip to the Ebro, where on the second day we had these lovely fish – a 139lb fish for me and John's first over 100lb (108lb). Both were caught on buoy-rigged livebaits, while being guided by Gary Allen.

Playing, Landing, Handling and Retaining Big Catfish

Hooking a big catfish of, say, over 100lb, is quite an experience and requires a level head and a steady nerve. The fish on the end of your line will be 6ft long minimum, extremely strong, and pretty unimpressed with the situation. Expect catfish to go (and stay) deep, so maintain a steady pressure. Put on a butt pad to prevent painful bruising. Check your clutch and be alert for potential danger spots, such as snags or rocky areas. If the swim is fairly clear, playing fish from the bank (rather than from a boat) puts you in better control and you are likely to land the fish more quickly.

Some fish will appear not to be very large and will come in fairly gently, until they realize what is going on and then the fun really starts. If you are concerned about snags close in and you have an adequate boat to hand you can play the fish from that; it will take longer as the boat will move much more than you think and the pressure on the fish will be less than it is from the bank. Make sure that there are two of you on the boat (assuming it is large enough). As with catfishing in Britain, expect to get heavy twangs on the line from the fish's tail as it whips round during the fight.

You can land fish from the bank by using big landing nets or by glove. If you are out on a river in a boat, large landing nets are not very practical: gloving is a more suitable method (*see* page 85), but remember to tap the fish on the head before gloving it to ensure that it is ready.

Hand-landing catfish on to a boat can be a fraught business. A friend of mine hooked a big catfish, and his companion (who had not previously seen a big cat) donned the gloves to land it. Unfortunately, when the fish's huge mouth came into view my friend's companion ran out of the water, up the bank, and refused to go near it, so the angler had to glove the fish himself.

To glove a catfish, grasp the lower jaw firmly, bearing in mind the position of the hook, and carefully pull the fish into the boat. The balance of the boat must be maintained if you are to

soft lures have also caught a number of fish. It is a method that you could use opportunistically if you see fish striking or if you are working your lure along the margins. The takes can be vicious since catfish are capable of fast, short-range lunges and aggressive takes. When filming for *Passport to Catfish: Spain* I had a take on a jigged rubber shad from a catfish estimated at just 10–15lb, but it hit so hard that I fell over. It was an incredibly hard bang on the rod just as the lure reached the edge, so it was on short line. I intend to do more lure fishing for catfish on future trips.

Stout pliers are recommended for unhooking catfish.

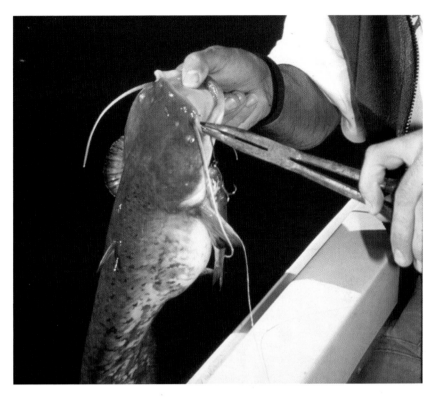

Spanish gold, the reason why so many journey to the Ebro – a chance of a beauty like this one, caught by Philip Bell-Scott.

A terrible sight but one that needs to be shown. This catfish had been left on a rope for days by a Spanish angler and was very unlikely to survive. When the angler left we cut the fish free.

avoid disaster, and make sure that you have a decent unhooking mat or some other padding in the boat.

Weighing and Measuring

A suitable weigh sling and a set of good scales are the ideal equipment for weighing fish. But if you do not have a sling, or your scales are inadequate, you can estimate its weight by measuring it. (The method for measuring catfish and estimating weight is described on page 89.) If you generally make a point of measuring catfish that you are also weighing in a sling, you will develop a good sense of how length equates to weight. Once you have caught a few catfish, a quick measure will give you enough of a size guide without your having to weigh every fish.

Retention

Fish should be released as quickly as possible: retain them only if you really have to. Great stress, not to mention physical damage, can be caused to fish that are inappropriately retained or retained for too long.

Catfish up to around 80lb may be retained in suitably sized catfish tubes in still water; for bigger fish, and for fish in rivers, stringers are the sensible option. Always be particularly careful when retaining big fish. Normally, if you put a fish out on a stringer it will swim away slowly, pull against the stringer for a couple of minutes, and then settle down and just lie quietly. If the fish does not settle, do not ignore it: distressed fish will not settle however long you leave them, and they should be released immediately.

8 THE FISH OF A LIFETIME

Enlightenment

I had never thought about catfish in my early years of fishing, though I was aware of them as I had developed an interest in keeping unusual coldwater species in aquaria and had already kept the American bullhead catfish and the channel catfish.

Wels catfish came significantly closer to me when, in 1983, I moved to Campton, a small village just outside Shefford in Bedfordshire. I had just started my first job and my route to work each day took me past a lake, although I wasn't aware that it was there until autumn came and I saw the glint of water through the thinning hedge. Being a keen angler, it took me only until the next weekend to visit the lake and start chatting to the anglers who were there. Soon into the conversation, one mentioned that there were catfish in the lake. From that moment on I was going to fish for them. The CCG was formed the following year; I joined and soon developed friendships with Kevin Maddocks and Bob Baldock. Bob gave me advice on the Airman Pit, which led to my first catfish capture. From then on, I was hooked on catfishing.

Soon the lure of big fish abroad saw us travelling, along with Keith Lambert, to many countries in search of bigger catfish. As a group, we caught some big fish, but I didn't land any really big ones. My biggest after many trips was an 84lb 8oz fish from the Saône. I hooked a couple of big ones (both almost certainly over 100lb), but lost them because the tackle we were using at that time was probably too light.

After some years of making these trips my family life took over as my children came along (three, each only 15 months apart), which

meant hard work and little fishing, and I stopped the trips abroad for a couple of years. It was pretty poor timing for me because this was the time at which we 'discovered' – or became aware of – the potential of the river Po in Italy. Catfishing, wherever you are in the world, is at its best when the fish have not been under pressure. The Po was one such water and, over the two-year period that I did not do any travelling, Kevin, Bob and Keith had some good results. Drifting and clonking had proved very effective, and they had a lot of catches to just over 100lb and the potential for bigger fish. I was desperate to try for them, and so, after lengthy negotiations with my wife, I secured a week's trip to Italy with Keith.

Italy

The week of the trip came and I flew out to join Keith, who had already been fishing there for a week with Richard Lopez. The timing of the trip had been set for the best period of the year, with a low chance of floods – which hit the river regularly in spring and early summer – and we were fortunate to have the local help of John Laing, a real character.

As soon as I arrived I was eager to hear reports of the state of the river and what had been caught in the first week. It seemed that the fishing had been tough – the river was fairly high and with some colour. Not many fish were responding to the clonk. The only sizeable one, a 65-pounder, had been caught by Richard that morning. 'Never mind lads, let's get out and have a go,' I said. I had been so starved of catfishing I was mad for it.

We set out that afternoon. All our fishing on the Po was by boat since the river is very big and powerful and couldn't be fished from the bank. As John was familiar with the stretch, we motored upstream about three miles to the first of the runs and the generally deeper water areas where the catfish lie under the current. The technique was to float-fish squid or livebaits (set at varying depths), drift down, and use the clonk to attract the catfish. An echo sounder was used to monitor the depths and to watch for catfish rising from the bottom in response. We managed to spot a few fish on the echo sounder, and Keith had one hit, which he missed, but things were much slower than we expected. I didn't mind as I was getting used to the technique and we had the rest of the week in which to fish.

At the end of the session we retired to John's *baracca*, a barge with corrugated iron shack and covered area. This was our base for the week. Spirits were high, and we enjoyed some wine and looked forward to the morning.

Dawn broke and I was woken early by the birds. When I got up, my jaw dropped. The river had risen 6ft overnight and was in spate, chocolate brown with branches, debris and even whole trees coming down, completely unfishable. I was devastated. All this time with no catfishing and now fantastic prospects washed away. The Po is a big river and can be affected in this way by rains hundreds of miles away, so, even though it was baking hot and clear where we were, somewhere upstream had experienced heavy rain some time previously. With nothing to be done in these conditions we sat on the bank for two days waiting, but the river did not change. We discussed our options. We could either wait longer or we could try the tributary close by, the Mincio, which also contains catfish. The Mincio is smaller, more like a big English river, but it would at least give us a chance of fish. We could boat fish in the day and put baits out at night. John went off for a couple of days' work, and we were left to try the Mincio.

We had two days and nights there, worked hard, and caught a lot of catfish clonking, but they were all small. We probably had 30 fish in two days, with none larger than about 20lb. However, the fishing had enabled me to get to grips with the methods, and at least we were fishing. On the third day we had a call from John, who said the main river was dropping and we should all meet back at the *baracca*.

When we met later that day I could see that the river was probably 4ft lower. It was still running pretty strongly, but the amount of debris in it had fallen, making it less hazardous for boat fishing.

We had one afternoon, a full day and a morning left. We fished that evening with no takes, and prepared for a big effort on the last full day. We were up early and fished hard until almost dark, but the conditions were still against us and, though we saw a few fish on the echo sounder, we couldn't get a take. I was gutted. We went off to a restaurant and had a splendid last-night meal, but I couldn't enjoy it as much as I should have done – I was just so desperate to get a decent fish.

We got up in the morning with aching heads to find that the river had dropped a little more, and I persuaded the others that we could fish for a couple of hours before packing and leaving. We got the boat sorted out and decided to try the big eddy at the end of the backwater where the moorings were. When I say it was an eddy, it was a 15-acre eddy, averaging 25ft deep with big branches and entire trees floating round and round: a surreal spot. We set up, float-fished livebaits, and drifted round the eddy. John did a little clonking, but not as much as he had done on the main river because we were covering the same area repeatedly. Nothing happened on the first couple of circuits, and so I adjusted my livebait to run through at about 18ft deep.

Success

As we drifted round on the next circuit, my float disappeared with a sharp 'plop' noise. Since I was already holding the rod, I struck straight away. It was like hooking a sandbag, of uncertain weight. As often happens with big catfish, the fish didn't really seem to know that

It was huge!

My fish of a lifetime.

known that it was really big but didn't want to make me more nervous. 'Should go a hundred pounds – take it easy.'

A hundred-pound fish! This was what I was so desperate to catch, but the fight was not over and I had to endure another ten minutes of losing and gaining line as I coaxed the fish to the boat. At this point, Keith tapped it on the top of the head, as you have to do to determine whether the fish is ready to be landed (*see* page 85). The fish turned away when tapped, so landing could not be attempted, but luckily it didn't go off too far and I brought it back a second time. This time, when tapped, the fish didn't move, so we knew it was ready. Keeping an eye on where the hook was, Keith grabbed the lower jaw using Kevlar grip gloves to protect him from the rasping teeth. I was still tense: the fish was still not in the boat. Keith leaned hard and hauled the fish out. Landing catfish into a boat is tough since most of the weight is at the front, but, once you have the head and belly over, the rest flies into the boat after it. In the boat the fish looked enormous and I just stood there shaking. 'It's a bloody big fish,' said John. 'We didn't want to say so in case you lost it.'

I just sat down in the boat, exhausted, and shed a few tears from pure emotion. I had been travelling abroad to fish for catfish for over ten years, hoping to catch my fish of a lifetime, and I'd just done it. The week had been so hard, and I'd missed catfishing so much that it was just a mass of feelings all at once.

Triumph

The short motor back to the *baracca* was a haze. We set up the big scales to weigh it. I measured it first – 7ft 4in (2.23m). Round went the scales, past 100, past 120, past 140. I couldn't take it in. 'Taking off the sling, it's 147,' said Keith.

It sank in: I'd just picked up the second largest cat ever caught by an English angler – total satisfaction after all those years of trying to catch a hundred-pound fish. After the many years of fishing abroad, my number had come

it was hooked: it stayed deep, towing the boat, after it. Thankfully, it stayed in the eddy and didn't venture out into the main flow, which would have been very hairy. After about five minutes the fish woke up and went steaming off. I was terrified of losing it – having previously, in Russia, lost a huge fish that I had played for over ten minutes. Every bang on the line (this is usually when the catfish's tail whips round and plucks the line) felt as if the fish had come off, giving me a sick-stomach feeling. I gradually managed to persuade and bully the fish up from deep water. 'Looks like a decent fish,' said Keith, who, I found afterwards, had

Red sky at night, catfisherman's delight.

up. After some photographs, we released the fish, packed up and, within 90 minutes of the capture, we had left the river to begin our journey home.

The actual capture was entirely owed to the help and guidance of Keith and John, and I shall always be grateful. Now, eight years later, I have only just beaten that record with a 155lb fish from Spain, but when I reflect on the Po fish – with the lead up, the condition of the river and the fight – it remains comfortably my best ever fish.

9 CATFISHING BEYOND EUROPE

While there is more than enough catfishing across Europe to keep any angler challenged for a lifetime, there are a lot more amazing catfish species around the world that really get the fishing juices flowing and offer some fantastic experiences.

Catfish anglers mostly like hard-fighting fish, and the catfish in warm water seem to fight even harder than the wels catfish, so you can be in for some arm-aching action.

There are big catfish to be caught from South America to Africa and right across the Asian continent – the world is your oyster. But where to start? I have yet to travel beyond Europe on a big catfish trip but my good friend Graham Lawrence has. Here he offers an insight into what is in store for the intrepid travelling angler.

Experiences with Tropical Cats

By Graham Lawrence

Having fished for wels catfish in Britain, I became interested in some of the other big catfish that can be found across the world. I have also been a keen aquarist for a number of years and in that time managed to obtain some of these

King of the African catfish: the vundu.

Along with the monster-sized catfish that are associated with exotic places around the world, there are thousands of smaller species; James Peacock displays one of the amazing armoured catfish of South America.

The vundu catfish of Africa; probably, pound for pound, the hardest fighting freshwater catfish in the world. It can be glove-landed like a wels.

unusual species (of very small size), which increased my fascination. Over the years this became an obsession, and I set about planning trips. I started in Europe, fishing for wels catfish, but stories of big catfish well beyond Europe soon drew me to broaden my horizons. I found out more and, during the last ten years, I have travelled to many countries in search of new species, stretching my finances beyond sensible boundaries and testing the unending patience and support of my wife, Jo.

The waters in which catfish are found are varied – from small, fast-flowing rivers, through huge lakes and small pools, to deep gorges. We, as anglers, still do not know all the waters and the fish that are out there. In fact, the fishing

spots are as varied as the fish. You could write a whole book about these, so here is a taster to give you a view of some of the fishing to be had and the main angling destinations.

Africa

The continent of Africa offers a real challenge. There are three main species that are fished for. The clarius cat – or the barbell (as it is known locally) – is a relatively small, widely distributed species; it can grow to about 30lb although it is more likely to be caught in the 6–10lb range. The sematundu cats, which usually inhabit river systems, can grow to around 100lb. But the grandfather of African cats is the vundu, which can grow to over 150lb. This may not be the best looking of fish but its fighting ability far outweighs the wels for sheer power and speed. There are also very large armoured cats in the Congo; little is known about them because this area of Africa is such a difficult and dangerous place to visit, but they are definitely on my list for the future.

A trip to Africa is one that requires preparation and much patience. Travel within it can be time-consuming, hot and dusty. Delays are almost inevitable, and luggage going astray is a depressingly regular occurrence. (One of the best pieces of advice I can give any travelling angler is to pack as much of his critical tackle as possible in his hand luggage. This can be difficult on international flights with strict restrictions on 'dangerous items' in hand luggage; but for internal travel abroad it is rarely an issue.) When you

are actually fishing, there are some dangerous creatures that you have to be wary of: crocodiles and hippos, the most dangerous river- and lake-dwellers, demand the greatest respect. However, the rewards derived from the angling and the beauty of the continent more than make up for some of these trying obstacles, and there are established quality fishing camps for those wanting reasonable comfort.

South America
South America has an extraordinary number of species of catfish, from very small to extremely large. Travelling to the Amazon basin involves more flights and travel links than most other destinations; you can expect three flights and lengthy river trips to reach the better fishing

James Peacock displays this beautiful red-tailed catfish.

The jau catfish of South America.

areas because poaching has decimated the populations of many big fish close to civilization. South America also has one of the most frustrating pests that affect catfishing: piranhas. Using live fish and deadbaits for catfish often becomes impossible when piranhas are in the area. The thing I most dread is casting out and seconds later seeing the float vibrate, bob for about five seconds, and then go still – for this means your

bait has been munched through by piranhas. You then have to reel in, replace the bait, and move to another spot in the hope that there are no piranhas there.

As well as the most dazzling variety of catfish, small and large, with some amazing colours, South America has some other prized big sport fish such as the arapaima and the golden dorado, along with many varieties of stingray. In most rivers, unless you are using really big baits, you hardly know what will take your bait next, such is the variety of fish present.

Starting at the top, the really big catfish of the Amazon are the jau and the piraiba, which both grow to well over 300lb. The jau is quite strange in that it is a sandy colour when small, turning black as it gets bigger. It is relatively widespread and many anglers have been able to catch it. The piraiba is a personal favourite, although I have yet to catch one. To me this is a truly stunning fish – striking blue in colour and with a head similar to that of a shovel nose. It is something of an enigma: scarcer than the jau, and migratory, it remains unseen and uncaught by most anglers.

Of the other large catfish species the red-tailed catfish is one of the most beautiful. You may well recognize it as it is a popular aquarium pet when small, easily identifiable by its vivid red tail and known for its eating abilities, but for South America this is merely a medium-sized cat which rarely exceeds 100lb. There are many shovel-nosed catfish species, all striking to look at; the main angling quarry is the pintardo, which is very long with grey on its back and white stripes or spots, again growing to a maximum of about 100lb.

In addition there are hundreds of small catfish species with various spotted and striped markings, some with very long fins and others with armoured plating and spines along their sides.

India

In India there are two main catfish species for the angler to target: the mulley and the goonch. The mulley is similar to the wels in body but it is grey in colour and has a bigger mouth; it grows to around 100lb. It has a liking for just about anything that moves in water so I think it would be a fun fish to catch. The goonch is one of the strangest catfish of all. This fish looks almost lost in time: it has a serpent-like face with teeth to match, and it is one of the most striking fish I have ever seen; to top this, it grows extremely large, to well over 200lb. It can live in very small rivers and has supposedly been known to take cattle as food. It is also said that

it feeds on the remains of cremations that take place along the riverbanks, which seems a more likely possibility.

Many Indian rivers are heavily poached, and dynamite is a commonly used tool, which kills indiscriminately. So, when you are fishing for fish that have grown to large size and are therefore likely to be over 20 years old, you need to choose your location carefully. Holy sites, reserves and national parks are the areas that are best protected from poaching, so these are the ones to target, but reaching the remote pools may involve some arduous trekking.

Trips to India are memorable in many ways and for many things – from the striking poverty in so much of the country to the most frightening minibus drive I have ever taken along a road full of completely mad drivers. India is also the place where you are most likely to get an upset stomach.

Thailand

In recent years Thailand has become a popular destination with anglers seeking big catfish. The largest, the Mekong catfish, can grow to over 500lb; the lean, long-barbuled swai catfish grows to 50lb; and the chao phraya catfish can attain 200lb.

As well as the rivers and lakes, there is some excellent fishing to be had at a new generation of commercial fisheries that contain huge fish not just from Asia but from North and South America. Thailand has long been at the centre of the aquarium fish trade and, with the increasing drive towards sourcing captive-bred (rather than wild-caught) fish, many species have been imported for breeding. The big fish species have naturally grown prodigiously, and many have been stocked into these commercial lakes. Catfish are among these.

At such venues you can sit and fish, while being brought breakfast or drinks, before retiring to a comfortable hotel. Although it is not personally attractive to me as an angling challenge, it does offer good sport for anglers who want to experience many different species and want to do so in relative comfort.

A prehistoric monster! This incredible goonch catfish was captured by the top international catfish specialist and all-round nice guy Arnout Terlouw.

Preparation and Vital Equipment

In addition to the considerations outlined by Simon for travelling to Europe, when travelling further afield there are additional factors that must be borne in mind.

Understand Your Destination

Depending on the remoteness of your destination and the nature of the trip, you are likely to require some special equipment and/or to have to take particular precautions before and during the trip.

There are now many well-established fishing destinations around the world that have good facilities and can offer reasonable comfort. For this type of destination, there are many angling travel companies that can offer advice on ap-

propriate equipment and preparation. But if you are planning a trip to one of the more remote locations, you may need to take account of, or make provision for, the following:

- Special travel requirements. For example, are visas required? (Some may take a long time to obtain.)
- Inoculations. Find out which ones are necessary for the destination. Check with your doctor well in advance as some are best taken months before you depart and, if you require several, they are often best spaced out.
- Weather conditions. You will need suitable clothing and footwear for wading and tropical climates.
- Equipment and tackle. You may need to take extra gear.

- Medical facilities. It may be that you will be travelling some distance from decent medical provision and therefore you might consider taking out special medical insurance and taking more than your usual medical supplies.
- Dangerous fauna and flora. In addition to having inoculations, take adequate protection and clothing.
- Accommodation and food. If you are going to be living in the wild take such items as mosquito nets, head nets and water-purifying tablets; these do not take up much room and may be essential.
- Travelling time and delays. The more remote your destination, the more complicated your travel itinerary is likely to be, increasing the likelihood of delays and the potential for lost luggage. Make sure you allow for this in the planning for your trip.
- The stability and security of your destination area. These factors require careful consideration and, since they can vary from time to time, it is important to obtain up-to-date information. For example, Zimbabwe used to be a popular destination, but travel there at the moment needs to be carefully evaluated in view of the political situation. Even in politically more stable regions, sensible travelling equipment, such as a money belt, may be recommended.

Methods

It has been surprising to find that much of the tackle and methods employed around the world are similar to those used for wels catfish. Most tropical catfishing involves fishing on the bottom with live or dead fish, offal or meat. Some species will take surface baits, mostly when they are actively hunting and can be seen chasing small fish on or near the surface. Depending on conditions, straightforward running leger or float-fishing outfits are the order of the day, with the same tackle as that used in Europe on the big rivers.

The strange feeding habits of some fish mean that unusual baits and methods can be used in some countries. For example, in Lake Kariba in Zimbabwe a well-known bait for vundu catfish is blue soap. It makes more sense than it first seems as the soap is made from animal fat. Locals say that women doing washing in the lakes have seen very large vundu attracted by the soap.

In India the goonch hunts very differently from any other catfish I have caught. It spends a vast amount of time static on the bottom of rivers and seems only to take a bait if it passes directly in front of its mouth; the bite may be seen as only a small knock on the rod tip. I think it would be fair to say that most people who have hooked a goonch didn't even know that it

Soap to catch catfish? The famous blue soap, which is animal-fat based, is one of the best vundu catfish baits. The soap is not readily taken by other species, so if you get a run it is almost certainly a vundu.

Super fish; John Wilson displays the hard-fighting Mekong catfish.

was there until they reeled it in. The Mekong cat of Thailand does not normally feed on anglers' baits; in the wild it feeds on plankton, but those stocked into lakes have been taught to take bread, so by using bread flake they can be caught on rod and line.

This has been a brief overview of what can be found around the world. So if you like catfish, but want to try something a little different, why not have a look at tropical cats? Who knows what is still swimming out there in remote rivers across the world? I'll still keep looking …

10 MORE ABOUT CATFISH

The Catfish Conservation Group

I believe it is fair to say that the Catfish Conservation Group (CCG) has been the catalyst for the growth of catfishing in Britain and the increasing numbers of British anglers travelling abroad for wels catfish. From humble beginnings, the CCG has become one of the main single-species angling groups for over 20 years and the major force in catfishing in the UK.

The CCG was formed in 1983 by anglers Bob Baldock, Kevin Maddocks, John Golder and Glyn Owen. At the time there were no more than a handful of waters containing wels catfish. Little was known or written about catfishing, yet there was growing interest from anglers and concern that catfish could be mistreated by anglers who might be nervous about handling them.

Its original aims are still in existence:

1. To promote the conservation of existing catfish stocks and to recommend correct angling methods, treatment and careful handling of the species.
2. To encourage fish farmers to breed the European catfish (wels) for the purpose of stocking English waters and to assist them wherever possible.
3. To negotiate, whenever necessary, with the water authorities for consent to stock catfish.
4. To encourage fishery owners and managers to stock the wels and to assist them in every possible legal way.

The Catfish Conservation Group is your best source of information about catfishing, and your shortcut to catching more fish; you can see them at most major fishing exhibitions.

157

This immaculate 33lb catfish was caught on a poly-balled livebait during a CCG fish-in at the Split lake, part of the famous Yateley complex.

5. To prove, to whomsoever it may be necessary, that the presence of wels does not significantly influence the stocks of other more popular species.
6. To compile as much information as possible about the life history of wels and make this information available to fish farmers.
7. To encourage more anglers to become interested in the wels and to develop the CCG into an international organization for friendship and cooperation between all catfish anglers.

At the time of the CCG's formation, it was unique in that even before it had been formally launched it produced a top-quality magazine. It

was a risk, but it paid off. In less than a year over a hundred members had signed up and, at the first CCG meeting (at Little Brickhill in autumn 1984), more than that number packed into the hall. The interest was obviously there, and it was clear that the group would be a success.

Progress to the Present
The beginnings of the CCG proved to be a sound base for successful growth. The work during 1984 and the ensuing years provided a catalyst for increased interest in a species about which so little was then known. The CCG set about running fishing meetings and attending shows to help spread the word. It met with water

authorities and English Nature and helped many anglers who wanted to know more. There was also a great interest from clubs and fisheries interested in stocking wels.

Owing to the short supply of stock fish, one of the CCG's main aims was to encourage British fish farmers to breed catfish. Unfortunately, even to this day there has been no commercial breed-ing of catfish in Britain. However, the stock sup-ply issue was well addressed by the late 1980s and the 1990s through the importing of good-quality fish from the Continent. The plentiful supply from countries such as Croatia was pri-marily owed to the large programme of farming wels catfish for food in many eastern European countries. The influx of this new stock provided

My first 30-pounder (32-00) was this long, lean fish from Wintons fishery. I was the last to arrive and took the only swim left; then I had the only catch – which was nice.

a considerable boost to the number of waters containing catfish and, since that time, as stocks have grown naturally, fisheries have supplied excess stock to supplement the imports and help towards meeting the demand for this fine sporting fish. As catfish have become more widely available, and the supply side has been largely addressed, the CCG has moved more towards helping anglers to fish for catfish through the provision of help and information.

Significant Steps

Since its formation, the CCG has launched several major initiatives:

- In 1990 the CCG leased and stocked its own catfish water: Adams Pool at Alcester, which continues to offer great catfishing at a reasonable price to members.
- In 1991 the CCG made the video *Catfish and How to Catch Them*, which has helped thousands of anglers to make their first catch.
- In 1996, the CCG Awards Scheme was created. With this scheme the nature of the lake is taken into account: in other words, it is acknowledged that captures are associated with the particular lake and that not all lakes contain huge fish. It is important to recognize this – to concede that captures of the biggest fish are not necessarily the catches of greatest merit. A lake-record fish is a lake record whether it is 20lb or 70lb.
- In 1997 the CCG published the first edition of the *UK Guide to Catfish Waters*, which listed over 170 waters containing catfish. This enabled anglers to locate nearby waters and gave helpful information about costs, stock, fishery direction, and so on. The second edition was published in 2005 and contained over 250 waters.
- In 2005 a new DVD *A Catfishing Season* provided an up-to-date look at methods, tactics and tackle for modern catfishing (replacing the original *Catfish and How to Catch Them* video. The DVD follows anglers through a season, with spring, summer and autumn sessions, and covers the different approaches and tactics that can be employed; this is ideal for anyone wanting to understand more about the methods in use.
- Since 1985 the CCG has run catfish 'fish-ins'. These have been the main summer activity organized by the CCG and have given much pleasure and assistance to anglers. The fish-ins started when there were few catfish available and the only place to fish was at Woburn Abbey lakes (which contained lots of catfish). The Shoulder of Mutton lake at Woburn Abbey could be rented by the day, although you were obliged to rent the whole lake (there was no option to rent only part of it). The cost was £65 – which in 1985 was not cheap. To begin with, informal bookings were taken from among a few members, but then the fish-ins were publicized through the CCG. Since then, the CCG has expanded the number of waters they visit. The aim is to have a 'catfishing first' session on several fisheries; in contrast to an average day on many fisheries, where you are most likely to have ten carp anglers for every catfish angler. By taking over an entire fishery there is a focused effort, maximizing the chances of cats being caught. At these events less experienced anglers can get help and the events have proved to be quite social. This has proved a good formula, particularly for the anglers who do not know many other cat fanatics. We are also able to fish several waters that are not normally open to day-ticket fishing.

Membership

The CCG has been well supported for its whole existence, with a strong membership base of well over 500, despite the relative shortage of catfish waters for most of its existence. It is an open group, welcoming all those interested in wels catfish, whatever their level of experience. Members receive the excellent annual *Whiskers* magazine and newsletters, and they can participate in the CCG Awards scheme, attend fish-ins and book the CCG fishery Adams Pool. Membership is currently just £13 annually; to join, contact the CCG (*see* Appendix II).

Catfish as a Stock Fish

Stocking wels catfish into lakes offers fisheries and angling clubs a good opportunity to provide an additional attraction to their fisheries. Many people who have not experienced catfish are sometimes nervous about stocking them and, when you consider some of the misleading articles in the press that have been written about catfish, I am hardly surprised. There are probably more inaccurate stories and rumours about catfish than about any other species in the country – monsters of the lake, fish-eating machines, the emptying of lakes and other rubbish. The plain fact is that the wels catfish makes an excellent addition to many fisheries.

In considering the stocking of any fish species, any owner or controller would normally ask:

• Will the stock fish attract anglers?
• Will the fish offer a good sporting quarry?
• Will the fish complement the existing fish stock?
• Are the stock fish a good investment?

The answer for wels catfish on all counts is yes.

Paperwork

As a non-native species, wels catfish are classified as a Category 2 ILFA (Import of Live Fish [England and Wales] Act 1980) species. As such, they can be stocked only into enclosed British stillwaters, subject to certain requirements, the primary one being that they must not be within a flood plain. If the enclosed stillwater has an outflow, then gravel traps or screens normally need to be fitted to make doubly sure that there is no risk of escape into river systems where control would be much harder.

As with the introduction of any non-native flora and fauna, the authorities must asssess the risk of the introduced species 'escaping' into an area where it cannot be controlled; they must be satisfied that this risk is low, and sure that there would be no impact on native flora and fauna. So if you are interested in stocking wels, you need to apply for a licence and complete the appropriate

ILFA paperwork. The application will then be considered, taking into account the regulations applying to the lake and the assessments submitted by other bodies. Input is sought from English Nature, the Environment Agency (EA) and CEFAS (the Centre for Environment, Fisheries and Aquaculture Science), the scientific arm of the EA.

English Nature assess the lake for any special circumstances, such as whether it is an SSSI (Site of Special Scientific Interest) for any of its flora, fauna, or geological features. It has been incorrectly stated that you cannot get permission if the lake is an SSSI. In fact, a site can be designated as an SSSI for any one of a wide variety of species or features; if, for example, it is a waterside plant that has warranted the designation, the presence of fish on the site would have no impact, so permission would not necessarily be refused.

The CEFAS and the EA provide additional input regarding the risk of any escapes and any other considerations. Once permission has been granted, the normal regulations for any fish movement then apply, in no way different from those governing any other fish movement.

Some catfish are present in waters that are not licensed. It is possible to obtain retrospective licences, but the EA have proved on several occasions to be rather difficult about licences and have pursued many fisheries about the removal of catfish. I have repeatedly lobbied the EA to take a balanced view about catfish licensing – the fish have been here for over a hundred years and there are still no established river populations. The simple fact is that a balanced, constructive, cooperative approach to the licensing of waters would result in fewer secret stockings and illegal fish movements, which are far more risky.

The Impact on Other Fish

Many people are nervous about stocking catfish because they do grow large and they are predatory; however, they are not invasive and, as far as I know, have never been solely responsible for a British fishery being 'emptied of other fish'.

Catfish can be difficult to draw or paint, but David Clarke really got it right in this picture.

Some people say, 'You would say that – you like catfish.' My answer is to ask them whether they know of any such problems in any of the 250 waters listed in the CCG guide (I do not).

Carp are far more invasive and, indeed, on the CCG's own water, Adams Pool, despite having a large catfish population, carp regularly overpopulate the lake, which results in the decimation of silver fish. Each time we have removed carp by netting, the following years have been excellent for silver fish populations. Other waters containing carp and catfish have sometimes had their populations of silver fish reduced, but this is more to do with the total fish biomass and the competitive nature of carp rather than catfish. I say this because, if you removed all the carp from those waters, the silver fish population would undoubtedly recover. Furthermore, catfish have proved far less of a problem than other introduced fish species that have repeatedly shown the ability to establish large populations – sun bleak, topmouth gudgeon, and even zander.

Catfish have bred in nearly every British fishery where they are present, but the success of the breeding is usually poor. Typically, many tiny catfish may be seen after breeding, but the number of those that grow to, say, 2lb in weight is very low. Why is this? I believe that there are two primary factors. First, there is the climate: the United Kingdom is at the very northern end of the wels catfish's range, and since their growth rate in the first two years is low they are not always strong enough to survive the winters. Second, pike and, indeed, large catfish will predate heavily on catfish fry and reduce the populations of small fish considerably. The degree to which catfish predate on their own seems to depend on the total biomass of fish in a lake – the higher the fish population, the lower the amount of natural food available, and the higher the level of predation. Of course, there are a number of waters where catfish have bred well, and good numbers of small fish grow to over 3lb, but this is uncommon. If catfish were to proliferate in fisheries, they can be removed easily by netting and then sold.

Stress in Transported Catfish

One important factor to remember when moving large catfish is that they can suffer badly from stress, particularly if they are held in tanks or other confined spaces for long periods. It is odd to consider that one of the toughest and most resilient fish in a lake can be so delicate when being transported. I think that the stress occurs mainly when the fish cannot find somewhere comfortable to lie up. An example of this can occasionally be seen when catfish are retained on stringers after capture: in most cases they will swim off and find somewhere to lie quietly, but sometimes they do not settle and I think that this causes them stress. Therefore, if you are moving fish, make a particular effort to minimize the time taken to do it and keep them in the dark if possible.

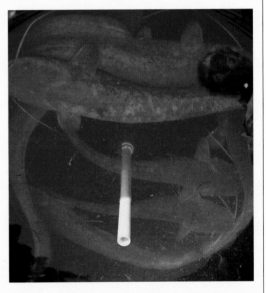

This consignment of catfish was part of the first stocking at the CCG's own water, Adams Pool, in 1992.

Disease Risk

With the significant growth of some nasty carp diseases reducing many fish populations, the risk of disease is always a concern. Catfish do not present any more of a health risk than most other fish, and certainly less of a risk than carp.

As far as I know, there has never been a fish kill as a result of a catfish introduction; not exactly what you could say about carp. However, as with any fish introduction, care should be taken to minimize risk and ensure fish welfare.

Plus Points

Catfish are predatory scavengers and thus useful to fisheries in mopping up dead and dying fish, anglers' bait, and nuisance species such as crayfish. Catfish are the only fish that have been shown to be able to control crayfish populations. Perhaps the EA should consider using catfish to exercise some control on non-native crayfish, which have affected many fisheries and proved almost impossible to remove.

Any fishery stocking catfish is likely to be making a sound financial investment: catfish remain in short supply (no one has yet been successful in breeding them commercially in Britain), and demand exceeds supply. If, in subsequent years, the catfish flourish and breed, surplus stock can easily be netted or rod caught for removal and sale.

Investing for the Future

There is one thing all catfish anglers can do and that is to continue to invest in the future of catfishing. If you have a local water that may suit catfish, work now to persuade the owners of the merits of catfish and to stock them. If you can get your local club to stock fish of a modest 5–8lb size you may expect that in just four years you could be fishing for 20lb-plus catfish, and they are likely to have bred.

I support the regulations preventing catfish from being introduced into river systems, but there is still plenty of room in British stillwaters for more catfish. If their availability were to be increased further, it would allow more anglers the privilege of encountering this fantastic fish.

Sourcing Tackle

In the course of running the CCG over the last 15 years I became aware that there was little specialist catfishing tackle available. What was avail-

After supplying catfish anglers with decent tackle by mail order, demand grew so much that I gave up my office job and set up Catfish-Pro to provide the top-quality, specialist tackle that catfish anglers deserve.

able was, for the most part, carp or pike gear and sea tackle for travelling abroad. At the request of many CCG members, I started to source catfish tackle some years ago and saw the range grow gradually. In 1984 I was approached by Leslies of Luton about supplying tackle to their shop. I supplied some items, which proved popular, and in the following year I decided to give up my office work and set up a specialist catfish tackle company: Catfish-Pro was born.

From the basic range that I had established I planned and developed a full range of tackle for sale through tackle shops. Producing a range ready for the shops was quite a challenge since I had previously been buying mainly wholesale in Britain and from abroad. I was able to develop some new sources and gradually improve the basics into a full range; this was complemented by the *CCG Guide to UK Catfish Waters* and the DVD *A Catfishing Season*.

The response from anglers has been overwhelmingly positive; however, the tackle shops have proved to be much harder to convince of the business potential of the range. The tackle market seemed to be just carp, carp, carp, and it has taken over two years to establish a reasonable set of stockists for the Catfish-Pro range. To find your local stockist or to request a brochure visit the Catfish-Pro website at www.catfish-pro.com or contact Catfish-Pro (*see* Appendix II for details). The range includes all you need to go catfishing, from starter kits and catfish rig kits, through rods, hooklinks, hooks, rig materials, to all the accessories for landing, unhooking and retaining catfish here and abroad.

Working on tackle and accessories full time has enabled me to talk to more catfish anglers,

Fish care is a duty for us all: catfish deserve proper catfish unhooking mats.

which has helped develop further products and accessories to enhance the range. Thus, with much effort and some laughs along the way, I have now planned, filmed and released two more catfishing DVDs: *Passport to Catfish: French Lakes* covers the tactics for lake fishing and is aimed at the many anglers travelling abroad, although it also has useful information on rigs and methods for Britain; and *Passport to Catfish: Spain, the Ebro*, which has been produced from trips to the top catfishing destinations and gives information on big river fishing, so different from lakes. On both I have tried to combine education and entertainment, with rig diagrams, information about methods, and plenty of catfish action.

I have been asked many times about a catfishing book to complement the DVDs and provide more detail than can be offered through a DVD. After a lot of effort, here it is.

More Information

If you are interested in getting into catfishing then there are a number of sources of help and information. The Catfish Conservation Group's website (www.catfishconservationgroup.com), contains information and articles. There are a number of other useful internet sites, though they can take some tracking down; the links page on the CCG website is a good place to start.

The 20th anniversary issue of the only dedicated catfish magazine in Europe: CCG's Whiskers; *unfortunately, our budget currently allows us to produce only one issue a year. Back issues are an excellent source of reading material.*

The CCG's annual magazine, *Whiskers,* is a mine of information: it includes the latest catfish waters list, venue records list, articles on rigs and methods, successful sessions and trips, and a lot more.

Any of the Catfish-Pro tackle stockists are a good place to seek information. Or, if you visit a water that has catfish, talk to the anglers and the fishery owners/controlling club to find out more.

It can also be worth visiting the various angling shows around the country. I and the CCG attend many of the main ones, so call by the stand for a chat if you are passing.

And if you really get stuck, give me a call on the CCG contact telephone number at the back of this book (*see* Appendix II).

And Finally ...

Fishing is a great hobby, enabling us all to get out to some lovely locations to fish in a relaxed or serious way. We have a good fishing community here and across the world. I hope you are as fortunate as I have been in my angling life, during which I have made many friends and had some laughs as well as memorable times. Maybe I'll meet you on the bank some day.

Good luck and good fishing.

APPENDIX I

BRITISH CATFISH WATERS

This list was kindly supplied by the CCG.

Bedfordshire

Airman Pit (Meppershall)
Arlesey Lake (Arlesey)
Beckerings Park Farm Reservoir
    (Steppingly)
Blue Circle Pit (Houghton Regis)
Browning Tingrith Coarse Fishery:
    Orchid Pool (Tingrith)
Hunters Moon Lake (Aspley Guise)
Husborne Crawley Lake (Coca-Cola's
    Lake) (Husborne Crawley)
Ivel Valley Fishery (near Broom)
Jones Pit and Little Jones Pit (Heath
    and Reach)
Medbury Lane (Elstow)
Priory Country Park (Cardington)
Rackley Hills Pit (Leighton Buzzard)
Radwell Complex: Sharnbrook Pit
    No. 2 (Sharnbrook)
River Great Ouse (Wyboston)
River Ivel (Lower Caldecot to
    Tempsford)
South Lagoon (Wyboston)
Tiddenfoot Pit (Leighton Buzzard)
Tingrith Manor Fishery (Tingrith)
Toddington Fisheries: Bottom Pool,
    Middle Pool (Toddington)
Westminster Pool (near Ampthill)
Withy Pool (Upper Stondon)
Woburn Estate Lakes: The Basin,
    Shoulder of Mutton Lake, Lower
    Drakeloe (Woburn Park)

Berkshire

Ashridge Manor (Wokingham)
Crayfish Pool (Horton)
Horton Boat Pool (Horton)
Horton Church Lake (Horton)
Orlitts Lake (Colnbrook)
Pondwood Fisheries: Lake One
    (White Waltham)

Buckinghamshire

Black Park Lake (Iver Heath)
Claydon Lakes: Lower Claydon, Middle
    Claydon (Middle Claydon)
Emberton Country Park: Snipe Pool
    (Emberton)
Furzton Lake (Milton Keynes)
Grand Union Canal: Aylesbury Arm
    (Simpson to Fenny Stratford, Marsworth to
    Hemel Hempstead)
Great Linford Lakes: Arboretum Lake,
    Blackhorse Lake, Parc Farm Two, Rocla
    (Little Linford)
Grebe Lake (near Calvert)
Len Gurd's Pit (near Woburn Sands)
Lodge Lake (Milton Keynes)
Mount Farm Lake [Beacons Pit] (Bletchley)
Old Slade Lane Lake (Richings Park)
River Ouzel (Stoke Hammond to Newport
    Pagnell)
Snowberry Lake (Little Brickhill)
Teardrop Lake (Milton Keynes)
Vauxhall Pits (Woburn Sands)
Weston Turville Reservoir (Weston Turville)
Willen Lake (Willen, Milton Keynes)

Cambridgeshire

Bainton Fisheries (Bainton)
Barnwell Pit (near Cambridge)
Barway Lakes: New Lake (Barway)
Bassingbourn Barracks: Longs Lake
  (Whaddon)
Burwell Lode (Burwell)
Colony Lake (near Manea)
Decoy Lakes (near Whittlesey)
Earith Carp Lakes: Pingree's Pool, Virginia
  Lake, Willow Walk (Earith)
Eggetts Lake (Hemingford Grey)
Fenland Fisheries: Willow Pool (Earith)
Gingerbread Lake (Eaton Socon)
Hartford Lake (Hartford)
Hemingford Grey Lake [L.A.A. Lake]:
  Hemingford Grey
Maxey Pit No. 4 (Maxey)
Northey Park Fishery: Blacketts, Pastsons
  Pool, Rio, Swallow Lake, Whiskers Lake
  (Peterborough)
River Great Ouse (Littleport, Little Paxton to
  Godmanchester)
Werrington Lakes (Werrington)
Willowcroft Farm Lakes: Catfish Lake
  (Wisbech St. Mary)

Cardiganshire

Celtic Lakes Resort (Lampeter)
Nine Oaks Fishery (Oakford)

Carmarthenshire

Castle Ely Fishery (Red Roses)

Cheshire

Brookside Fishery: Linear Lake (Higher
  Whitley)
Burton Mere Fishery: Burton Mere, Woodland
  Pool (Burton, near Puddington)
Crabmill Flash (Moston Green)

Dukes Pool (Sandbach)
Founders Pool (near Antrobus)
Grimsditch Mill Pool (Higher Whitley)
Home Farm Fishery: Coral Lake, Home Farm
  1, Home Farm 2, Juniors Lake (Alsager)
Lakemore Country Park: Horseshoe Lake,
  Long Lake, Willow Lake (Winterley)
Lymm Dam (Lymm)
Lymmvale (Marton)
New Pool (Higher Whitley)
Pickmere (Marston)
Plex Flash (Moston Green)
Rixton Clay Pits (Warrington)
Ruddy Pond (Dodlestone)
Shackerley Mere (Allostock)
Spring Pool (Higher Whitley)
Whitley Pool (Higher Whitley)

Clwyd

Sontley Pools (Middle Sontley)

Cornwall

Whiteacres Country Park: Nelson's Pool, Pat's
  Pool (White Cross)

County Durham

River Wear (Durham)
Tursdale Pond (Tursdale, near Coxhoe)

Cumbria

Lonsdale Park: Reed Mere (Cumwhinton,
  near Carlisle)

Derbyshire

KJS Fishery (Killamarsh)

Devon

Anglers Eldorado: Mixed Lake (Halwill)
Anglers Paradise: Easy Access Lake, Main
  Lake, Octopussy Lake, Specimen Carp Lake
  (Halwill)
Clawford Vineyard: JR's Lake, Major John's
  Lake (Clawton)
Oaktree Fishery: Stags Lake (West Anstey)
Stafford Moor Fishery: Joseph's Lodge
  (Dolton)
Valley Springs (Sherford)

Dorset

Revels Coarse Fishery: Specimen Lake
  (Buckland Newton)
Todber Manor (Todber)

Essex

Belhus Woods Country Park: Figure of Eight
  Lake (Aveley)
Birds Green Lakes: Home Lake (Birds Green)
Brock's Farm Fishery: Specimen Lake (Stock)
Bulphan Park Fishery (Burrows Farm)
  (Bulphan)
Carpenwater (Tendring, near Clacton-on-Sea)
Chigborough Fisheries: May Water, Scraley
  Mere (Heybridge)
Churchgate Lakes: Middle Lake
  (Battlesbridge)
Churchwood Fisheries: Churchwood Lake,
  Jenkins Lake (Doddinghurst)
Claverhambury Lakes (Waltham Abbey)
Crow Green Fishery: Main Lake, Syndicate
  Lake (Crow Green)
Crown Netherall Fishery (Lower Nazeing)
Crowsheath Fishery (Downham)
Dead Oak Fishery: Main Lake (Crays Hill)
Donylands Lake (Snake Pit) (Fingeringhoe)
Eweny Farm (The Ditch) (Southminster)
Forty Acre Plantation Lakes: Small Lake,
  Large Lake (Stock)
Fox Mere (Ulting Wick)

Fryerning Carp Farm Fisheries (Fryerning)
Green Lane Farm Fishery (Weeley)
Henham Lodge (Henham)
Hill Farm (South Ockendon)
Houchins Reservoirs: Back Reservoir, Front
  Reservoir (Coggeshall)
Jimmy's Lake (Corringham)
Lakeside (West Thurrock)
Maggits Lake (Basildon)
Marks Hall Fishery (White Roding)
Mollands Lane Lake [The Square] (South
  Ockendon)
Newlands Hall Fisheries: Osiers Lake, Moat
  Lake (Roxwell)
Noak Bridge Fishery (Billericay)
Oak Lodge Fishery (Rayleigh)
Old Hall Lake (Wakes Colne)
Olivers Lake (Witham)
PAR Fishery (near West Horndon)
Pea Lane Fishery (South Ockendon)
Slough House Lake (Bulphan)
The Pits Syndicate (near Clacton)
The Warren (Stanford Le Hope)
Tiptree Reservoir (Tiptree)
White Lakes: The Catfish Lake, The Carp
  Lake (Mayland)
Whittles Syndicate (White Colne)
Woody's [formerly Cobblers Mead]
  (Corringham)

Gloucestershire

Carp Society Horsehoe Lakes Complex: Lake
  61 (South Cerney)
Wildmoor Waters (South Cerney)

Greater London

Albyn's Farm: Tit Lake (Hornchurch)
Berwick Ponds (Rainham)
Brigadiers Lake (Woolwich)
Burgess Park Lake (Camberwell)
Canada Water (Southwark)
Little Britain Lake (Uxbridge)
Lizard Lake (West Drayton)

Manor Farm (North Ockendon)
Mayfields Lake (West Drayton)
Metropolitan Police Lakes (West Drayton)
River Thames (Hampton, Kingston,
    Twickenham)
Rookery Lake (Bromley)
Thamesmere (Thamesmead)
Valence Park Moat (Dagenham)
Wansted Golf Club: The Basin (Wanstead)
West India Docks (Isle of Dogs)

Greater Manchester

Debdale Reservoir (Gorton)
Giants Seat Fishery (Radcliffe)
Loonts Lake (Sharston)
Sale Water Park (Sale)
Taylor Pit (Shevington)

Gwynedd

Llyn Pentre Bach (Llanaelhaearn)
Llyn-y-Gors: The Carp Lake, Thompsons
    Lake (Llandegfan, Anglesey)
Pwll Helyg (near Caernarfon)
Pwll Ruddbysg (near Caernarfon)

Hampshire

New Forest Water Park (North Gorley)
Yateley Complex: Match Lake, Nursery Lake,
    Split Lake (Yateley)

Hereford and Worcester

Docklow Pools (Docklow)
Shatterford Lakes: Eric's Pool, Gainsborough
    Lake, Masters Lake, Stuart's Pool
    (Kidderminster)

Hertfordshire

Ashley (formerly Abbey Cross A.C. Pit)
    (Turnford)
Bayford Lake (Bayford)
Holwell Court Lake (Essendon, near Welwyn
    Garden City)
Manor House Farm (Wormley)
Slipe Lane Consortium Pits: Marsh Pit
    (Turnford)
Stanborough Park: South Lake (Welwyn
    Garden City)
Tring Reservoirs: Marsworth, Startops,
    Wilstone (Tring)
Willows Farm Fishery (formerly Bowman's
    Farm): Deep Lake (London Colney)

Kent

Barden Park (Tonbridge)
Cackle Hill Fishery (Biddenden)
Darenth Fishing Complex: Big Lake, Long
    Lake (Darenth)
Elphicks Fishery: North Lake, Plantation
    Lake, Prairie Lake (Horsmonden)
Green Acres Fishery: Specimen Lake
    (Biddenden)
Hawkhurst Fish Farm: Main Lake, Specimen
    Lake (Hawkhurst)
Hookstead Lakes: Charlie's Lake (Kingsnorth)
Manor Fisheries: Specimen Lake 2
    (Headcorn)
Mid-Kent Fisheries: Chilham Lake (Chilham)
Monk Lakes: Mallard Lake [Specimen Lake]
    (Marden)
Somerhill Fishery (near Tonbridge)
Springwood Fisheries: Carp Pool (near
    Flimwell)

Lancashire

Alkali Water Big Flash (near Preesall)
Bailrigg Lake (Scotforth)
Beacon View (Appley Bridge)

Borwick Fishing: The Last Blast (near
    Carnforth)
Fell View Lake (Goosnargh, near Preston)
Hudson's Farm (St. Michaels-on-Wyre)
Lyndhurst Fishery (Longridge)
Pendle View Fisheries (Barrow)
Wyreside Fisheries (St. Michaels-on-Wyre)
Wyreside Lakes Fishery: Banton Lake
    (Forton)

Leicestershire

Navies Pits (Wigston Magna)
Spring Grange Fisheries: Top Lake (Beeby)
Welham Lake (Welham)

Lincolnshire

Cleethorpes Country Park (Cleethorpes)
Daiwa Manton Pool (Manton)
Holme Fishery (Holme)
Lakeside (Cleethorpes)
Lakeside Leisure: The Boating Lake (Chapel
    St. Leonard's)
Langdale Lakes: Lily Lake (Langworth)
Messingham Sands Lakes: North Pool, South
    Pool (Messingham)
Oasis Lakes (North Somercoates)
Seven Lakes Country Park (Crowle)
The Nest (Winteringham)
Wagtail Lodge Fishery (Marston, near
    Grantham)
White House Predator Lake (Baston Fen)
Willow Bank Fisheries (Kirton in Lindsey)
Woldview (near Louth)

Merseyside

Sefton Park Lake (Liverpool)
Mid-Glamorgan
Maes Gwyn Fishery (Tonypandy)

Norfolk

Camelot Lake (Wortwell)
Cobbleacre Park Lakes (Hevingham)
Costessey Pits (Costessey)
Fendicks Fisheries: Small Pit, Medium Pit,
    Large Pit (Northwold)
Lakeside (Great Witchingham)
Nar Valley Fisheries: Fenn Lake, John's Lake
    (Pentney)
Pentney Lakes [Willowcroft Fisheries]: Cabin
    Lake (East Winch, near Pentney)
River Bure (Wroxham)
Swangey Lakes (West Carr, near Attleborough)
Taverham Mills Lake (Taverham)
Waveney Valley Lakes: Marsh Lake, Yew Tree
    Lake: Wortwell

Northamptonshire

Barby Mill Pools: Pool 2 (Barby)
Bluebell Lakes: Kingfisher Lake, Swan Lake
    (near Tansor)
Corby Boating Lake (Corby)
Foxholes Fisheries: Orchard Lake (Crick)
Lakeside View (Syresham)
Pitsford Fisheries [CCG Water] (Pitsford)
Ringstead Carp Fisheries: Crackers Meadow,
    Ringstead Carp Fishery (Ringstead)
Stanwick Lakes Fisheries: Elson's Lake
    (Higham Ferrers)

Nottinghamshire

Covert Springs Fishery (Woodborough)
Cromwell Lake (Cromwell, near Newark)
River Trent (Cromwell Lock)

Oxfordshire

Linch Hill Fishery: Stoneacres, Willow
    (Stanton Harcourt)
Milton Pools Farm Fishery: Specimen Lake
    (Great Milton)

Orchid Lakes: Club Lake (Dorchester)
Richworth Linear Fisheries: St. John's Pool
(Stanton Harcourt)
Vauxhall Pit (Stanton Harcourt)

Shropshire

Bache Pool (near Ludlow)
Bayliss Pools (Shifnal)
Blue Pool (Telford)
Hawk Lake (Hodnett)
Holmer Lake (Stirchley)
Middle Pool (Trench)
Poole Hall Fishery: Abbey Pool (Alveley)
Randlay Pool (Telford)
Townsend Fisheries (Alveley
Withy Pool (Dawley)

Somerset

Edney's Fishery (Mells, near Frome)
Parrots Paddock Farm (Nunney Catch, near
Frome)

South Glamorgan

Hazel Court Ponds (Llysworney)
Staffordshire
Browning Cudmore Fishery: Edwards Lake
(Whitmore)
Chasewater Country Park: Chasewater (near
Brownhills)
Meadow Lane (Burton-on-Trent)
Pool Hall Fishery (Trescott)

Suffolk

Cross Drove Fishery (Hockwold)
Homersfield Lake (Homersfield)
Lakeside (One House)
River Waveney (Beccles)
12 Acre Lake (Saxmundham)

Surrey

Badshot Lea Ponds: Large Pond (Badshot Lea)
Basingstoke Canal (Woking to Brookwood)
Beaver Farm Fishery: Main Lake, Snipe Lake,
Tuscany Lake (Newchapel)
Brittens Pond (Jacob's Well)
Kingsmoor Lake (Staines)
Red Beeches (Haslemere)
River Thames (Molesey Weir, Staines to
Sunbury, Upper Tidal)
Send Lakes: Cobbetts Lake, Sanderson's Lake
(Send, near Woking)
Stillwater (Ash Vale)
Stubpond Fishery: Forge Lake (Newchapel)

Sussex

East
Falkenville Fisheries (Mushroom Farm): The
Racetrack (Hailsham)
Framfield Park: Burywood Lake (Framfield)
Rye Nook (Rye Harbour)
Tanyard Fishery: Specimen Lake 3 (Furners
Green)
White Cottage Lake (Ripe, near Lewes)
Wishing Tree Reservoir (Hastings)

West
Furnace Lakes Fishery: Kiln Lake, Plantation
Lake, Roman Lake, Specimen Lake
(Slinfold)
Wintons Fishery: Mallard Lake, Kingfisher
Lake, Heron Lake (Burgess Hill)

Tyne and Wear

Mount Pleasant Lake (Washington)

Warwickshire

Adam's Pool [C.C.G. Water] (Alcester)
Napton Reservoir (Napton on the Hill)
Weston Lawns Fishery: Pool No.2 (Bedworth)

West Lothian

Eliburn Reservoir (Livingston)
West Midlands
Himley Hall Great Lake (Himley Park, near
    Dudley)
Lavender Hall Fisheries (Berkswell)

Yorkshire

East

Barton Broad (Barton-upon-Humber)
Emmotland Ponds [formerly Langholme Hill
    Fisheries]: Lake One, Lake Two (North
    Frodingham)
Fossehill Lakes [Humberside Shooting
    Ground]: Pond Two (Brandesburton)
Greaves End Pond (Eastrington Common,
    near Howden)
Greengrass Park Fishery (Hempholme)
Leven Park Lake (Leven)
Motorway Pond (Newport)
Oakland Waters (Gowdall)

North

Carpvale Pools: Cyprio Pool, Match Pool
    (Moor Monkton, near York)
Elvington Lake (Elvington)
Grafton Mere Fishing Lakes: The Carp Lake
    (Grafton)
Kingsley Carp Lake (Harrogate)
Newhay Lakes (Cliffe)
Rosedale Fishery (Hunmanby)
The Willows Fishery: Ridge Pool (Hessay, near
    York)

South

Crookes Valley Park Lake (Crookesmoor, near
    Sheffield)
Hayfield Lakes (Auckley, near Doncaster)
Stubbs Hall Lakes (Hampole)

West

Hopton Waters (Mirfield)
Knotford Lagoon (Otley)
Millrace Ponds (Garforth)
Sally Walsh's Dam (Kinsley)

APPENDIX II

USEFUL CONTACTS

The Catfish Conservation Group

The Retreat,
Heath Lane,
Ewshot,
Farnham,
Surrey GU10 5AW
www.catfishconservationgroup.com

Specialist Suppliers and Government Agencies

Catfish-Pro Ltd
www.catfish-pro.com
(Suppliers of specialist catfishing tackle.)

Biopharm
www.biopharm.co.uk
(Suppliers of medicinal leeches.)

The Environment Agency
www.environment-agency.gov.uk

DEFRA
www.defra.gov.uk

Travel and Guiding Services

Spanish Guiding Services

Catmaster Tours
www.catmaster.com

Catfish Capers
www.catfishcapers.co.uk

Bavarian Guiding Service
www.spanish-catfish-ebro.com

Catfish Connections
www.catfishconnections.co.uk

Ebro Views
www.ebroviews.co.uk

Publications

Whiskers
(Catfish Conservation Group; various issues 1984–2007)

UK Guide to Catfish Waters
(Simon Clarke and Paul Holroyd, for the Catfish Conservation Group)

INDEX